SETTING UP A BUSINESS

Vera Hughes and David Weller run their own business, DEVA Training Services, in Andover, Hampshire. Vera Hughes has also written *Teach Yourself Word Processing* and, with her daughter, *Teach Yourself The Office Handbook*.

TEACH YOURSELF BOOKS

SETTING UP A BUSINESS

Vera Hughes and David Weller

TEACH YOURSELF BOOKS

British Library Cataloguing in Publication Data

Hughes, Vera, *1936–*
   Setting up your own business.
   1. Great Britain. Small firms. Organization
   I. Title   II. Weller, David
   658′.022′0941

ISBN 0 340 50540 0

First published 1990 as *Setting Up Your Own Business*.
Reissued 1992 as *Setting Up a Business*

Impression number	15	14	13	12	11	10	9	8	7
Year		1999	1998	1997	1996	1995	1994		

Typeset by Rowland Phototypesetting Ltd, Bury St Edmunds, Suffolk.
Printed in Great Britain for Hodder & Stoughton Educational, a division of Hodder Headline Plc, 338 Euston Road, London NW1 3BH by Cox & Wyman Ltd, Reading, Berks.

Acknowledgements

The authors gratefully acknowledge the help and expertise of these people:
Tony Adams on all matters to do with the work of an Accountant; Bromley Public Library for its excellent reference section and helpful librarians; John Bucklow of VFM for his advice on marketing; Christina Hughes on all legal matters, particularly registered charities; Mary James for her experience of nannies and childcare; Cherry Mill for her help with personnel matters when employing others.

About the authors

Vera Hughes and David Weller started their own business, DEVA Training Services, in 1980 and expanded into word processing services and training under the name of DEVA WP in 1983. Before that they were involved in the retail industry for many years, and Vera became a Senior Training Advisor with the Manpower Services Commission (now the Training Agency), specialising in office and retail training.

They run their business as a Partnership and have experienced all the rewards and traumas of setting up and running a very small business. Vera and David have written a number of books on retailing, published by Hodder and Stoughton and Macmillan.

Contents

	Page
Introduction	xi

1   The First Step   1
Is it saleable?
  A sound product or service; The market need; Suppliers
Can you sell it?
  Personal attributes required; Self motivation;
  Organisational ability; Management of time; Energy and
  health; Communications skills; Pilot scheme

2   Money   11
Costing the product or service
  Cost price; Mark up and margin; Selling price
Working Capital and Cash Flow
Making a business plan
Presenting your case for funding

3   Premises   19
Working from home
Workshops, warehouses and factories
Office premises
Finding out what is available
Support and grants

4   Methods of Trading   30
Sole trader

Partnership
Limited company
Franchise
Co-operative
Registered charity
Multi-level marketing

5 **Marketing** 39
Your marketing profile
Marketing methods
    Advertisements; Mailshots; Leaflet drop; Printing and
    artwork requirements; Leads and personal contacts
Marketing your consultancy
Image
    Premises; Vehicles; Telephone; Letters; Advertising matter;
    Personnel

6 **Selling the Product or Service** 52
Preparation
The approach
Establishing the customer's needs
Features and benefits
Objections
Closing
Additional sales and services

7 **Doing the Books** 62
Receipts and payments
Petty cash
VAT
Banking
Necessary or useful records
Manual or computer
Year end

8 **Personal Finances and Business Expenses** 75
Money for personal use
NI contributions and pensions
Income tax
Allowable business expenses

9 **The Professionals**   82
How to find them
Accountants
Architects
Banks and building societies
Estate agents
HM Customs and Excise (VAT)
Insurance brokers
Printers
Secretarial services
Solicitors

10 **The Office**   91
Stationery
Business documents
    Estimate; Quotation; Order; Invoice; Credit Note;
    Statement; Remittance Advice; Letters
Computer or not?
    Hardware; Software; Materials; Suppliers
Telecommunications
    Telephones; Fax; Telex, Teletex and Electronic Mail
Furniture and equipment
Health and Safety at Work Act 1974

11 **Employing Others**   114
Staff recruitment
    Advertising; Selection; Interviewing
Pay
    Methods and frequency of payment; National Insurance;
    Tax and SSP; Maternity rights and pay; Pensions; Holiday
    pay; Sick pay
Contract of employment
    Main requirements; Disciplinary procedure; Periods of
    notice
Insurance
HASAWA
    Employer's obligations; Policy statement; Accident book;
    First aid
Data Protection Act

Do you need to register?; An employee's rights
Staff training
    Induction training; Further training

12 Opening a Shop   127
Siting
Image
Stocktaking
People
Legal requirements
Money
Security
Advertising

13 Import and Export   142
Import
    Ordering from abroad; Documentation; Clearing goods
    through customs and transportation; Methods of payment;
    Insurance
Export
    Should you export? Where to get help

14 Specially for Women   150
Running a home and a business
Children and other dependents
Your health
Your business image
Money
Women's organisations and training

15 Help and Advice   168
Local sources of help and advice
    Job Centres, Enterprise Agencies, Colleges, Banks and
    building societies, Public libraries
Useful addresses
Useful books and leaflets

Index   173

Introduction

Thinking of starting your own business? Just under way with your own business and wondering what to do next? Then this book is for you. It contains the usual advice you would expect to find in a book of this sort, but it also contains very practical hints from two people who have done it all themselves.

When you are starting to set up your own business, there are many things you need to know all at once, so to read this book from start to finish is not necessarily what you need. Each chapter is an entity in itself. For example, if you need to home in on marketing, or the office, all the information is in that chapter. You can dip in to a chapter, or even part of a chapter, for the parts which concern you. Consequently you will find repetitions in some chapters of the ideas put forward elsewhere; this is done deliberately. There are also cross references so that you can find the detail you need.

Use the contents pages and the index to find the points which really concern *you*. Use the final chapter as a reference for where to go for help. And good luck with your business venture!

Vera Hughes and David Weller

1

The First Step

In this Chapter
Is it saleable?   *A sound
   product or service; The
   market need*; *Suppliers*

Can you sell it?   *Personal
   attributes required; Self*

*motivation; Organisational
ability; Management of
time; Energy and health;
Communication skills;
Pilot scheme*

The first thing anyone needs before setting up any kind of business is an idea, or perhaps more precisely *the* idea of starting in business at all. It sometimes happens in a blinding flash, but more than likely it insinuates itself and gradually the idea of setting up a business develops until it is hard to remember when it was not there.

Before the idea takes over too much, certain questions need to be asked in order to keep things realistic and in proportion – not to kill off the idea, but rather to have a controlled development of it.

Is it saleable?

A sound product or service
The first question to ask about your idea could take the following form: *What precisely is the product or service I am going to offer?* followed by the key question: *Why should customers buy MY product or service rather than those which exist already?*

There is a distinct advantage if the product you are intending to offer is a legal requirement, in the sense that, potentially, you have a captive market. Items related to health and safety, for example, fire extinguishers or even Fire Exit and other related statutory signs would come into this category. You can probably think of other areas which could apply.

Nevertheless that key question still needs to be answered, and *answered realistically: Why should customers buy* MY *product or service rather than those which exist already?*. Make a list of the good points about your product – they could form the basis of your marketing strategy.

The market need
Continue to question your idea:

- *How many people are likely to want to buy my product or service?*
- *Will the numbers be sufficient to justify my proceeding with the idea?*
- *What competition already exists?*
- *How well established is it?*
- *Will I be able to compete?*
- *Is there a particular segment which I could concentrate on?*
- *Is what I am considering generally an expanding or a contracting market?*

The finding of the answers to these and other related questions forms the basis of the market research exercise which is necessary at this early stage to turn a hunch or idea into something more down-to-earth and practical, or to confirm that the original idea is sound.

As a small trader or partnership, you cannot afford to embark on a very large market research exercise, but it is worthwhile trying to establish whether what sells well to friends and colleagues will be bought by the public at large. The Kogan Page publication *Do Your Own Market Research* is very helpful.

The Training Agency runs market research courses for people starting up in business. Ask at your Job Centre, your local Enterprise Agency or your local college to see what courses are available. The courses include not only market research, but marketing, book-keeping, selling and many other matters dealt with in this book. A book can give you useful general guidelines – a course tutor can give you personal attention and expertise.

Suppliers
If your business idea involves selling a product, you will need to obtain either the raw materials which you are going to transform into something else, or the components which will create your finished article.

These items will need to be obtained from suitable suppliers. You will find that there is no shortage of people wanting to sell you things for your business. What you must do is draw up your product specifications very carefully and decide on the suppliers (and it is probably better to have more than one source) who will provide that quantity and the *quality* you need at the price you wish to pay.

Make a list of the components you need, and for each component write down the potential suppliers, their prices, delivery dates, settlement terms and product quality. Making such a list helps you to think clearly and objectively.

Can you sell it?

Personal attributes required
The personal attribute most required is belief in the product or service you are about to sell. If you do not have absolute faith in your product or the quality of your service, you will never get your business off the ground.

You must try not to be put off if other people's reactions do not initially match your enthusiasm.

Self motivation
The belief in your product or service is the first step in self motivation; what follows depends on your own ability to move off the starting line and keep up the momentum.

Sometimes people feel that those who have their own businesses are lucky, because they can suit themselves whether they work or not. To a certain extent this is true, of course: if you decide one morning that you would rather stay in bed than turn out in the cold to sell your product or service, that is up to you – your competitors will be delighted!

Self motivation is an attitude of mind as much as anything, and your attitude must at all times be to develop your business. If you are a sole trader this can be more difficult, since you may not have anyone else to help you with your motivational process. So self motivation should perhaps be coupled with self discipline. Determine to set yourself a regular business routine, and do all you can to keep to it. As you achieve this regular routine, you will find that your self motivation improves dramatically. There is nothing like a successful meeting or telephone call to stimulate motivation – the hard work is the initial effort needed to arrange that meeting or make that telephone call in the first place.

Organisational ability
There are people who scorn those who use personal organisers, dismissing them as a fad, but an absolute requirement of anyone who starts a new business is the ability to operate in an organised way. You cannot work effectively in a muddle.

This has nothing to do with the workshop with wood shavings on the floor, or even the desk with papers strewn over it. This is the ability to know when and where the next appointment is, of having a system to pick up messages periodically, of dealing with correspondence quickly and efficiently, of being able to put your hand on specific pieces of information promptly and responding effectively to queries or enquiries.

This is all part of self discipline which, as we have just seen, is also part of that all-important self motivation.

Management of time
Whether you are the chairman of an international business organisation or a sole trader, the amount of time available to you is exactly the same: there are precisely 24 hours in the day for both parties.

How those 24 hours are utilised is where the differences arise. Chairmen of multi-nationals probably have other people around them to ease the pressure on their time, while the sole trader more than likely has no such luxury, or at best very limited help. The management of available time effectively is therefore significant, requiring, once again, a high degree of self discipline.

One of the greatest causes of the mis-management of time is the very human one of doing those things which we want to do. One can always find a valid reason for putting off the unpleasant job.

Consider the following checklist – select those which are your most important ones *now*:

50 Time Management Guidelines: for people setting up their own business

PLANNING

1 Plan your time; do not let it control you
2 Assess your work – projects, tasks, etc. – and allocate priorities
3 Arrange and allocate your priorities into categories A, B, C and D
4 Throw away the Ds
5 Keep the Cs to be read during non-priority time
6 Date and/or time check the Bs: they are usually important but not urgent
7 Sub-prioritise your As – A1, A2, A3, etc.
8 Do the A1s *now*, then your other As – not those attractive Cs!
9 Chop the big task down into smaller, more manageable pieces
10 Estimate the finishing time for a task, not just the starting time
11 Always ask the questions: What? Who? Where? Why? When? How?

OPERATING

12 Use the 'To Do' system
13 Have a daily 'To Do' list – particularly for your A items
14 Review your daily list, first thing in the morning or last thing in the evening, and plan your priorities
15 Keep your daily 'To Do' list always in sight
16 As you clear each item, delete it in brilliant red – just looking at a list of completed tasks makes you feel even better!
17 Do not include too many items – remember the jobs which always crop up unexpectedly
18 Maintain a second 'To Do' list for longer-term tasks or those to which a date cannot yet be given
19 Transfer items from the second list to the daily list whenever relevant

20 Use the 'To Do' lists, do not ignore them – they are probably your most powerful time management tools
21 Write it down: do not try to keep your 'To Do' lists in your head – keep that free for actually doing them!
22 Leave some time for the unexpected
23 Have the things you need constantly to hand in one place
24 Identify and concentrate on the high-yield tasks if you have the choice

TELEPHONE CONTROL
25 Master your telephone techniques
26 Plan your telephone calls: use telephone 'To Do' lists as telephone agendas
27 If possible, arrange a specific 'call back' time – do not just say 'I'll ring you later' or, even worse, 'You ring me later'
28 If interrupted during a task by a telephone call, before answering pencil in your next thoughts. When you return to your task you will know what you were going to say next
29 Cross-index your telephone directory: name as one entry, organisation as the other
30 Quickly get to the purpose of the call: it is pleasant to socialise (gossip?), but it wastes a lot of time
31 Make sure you get the call-back name and number correctly: do not hesitate to ask for information until you have got it right

DISCIPLINE
32 Time management is 99% self discipline
33 Do the unpleasant task first, or as early as possible, particularly if it is your A1. It is most people's experience that these tasks usually turn out to be less unpleasant than was anticipated
34 Use the recommended time management techniques: they have been proved to work
35 Learn to say 'No'
36 Make sure you do it right first time: every time you have to re-try, you are wasting time
37 Avoid procrastination: get on with it
38 Set yourself personal deadlines for most tasks and stick to them if at all possible
39 Stick to the task you know *must* be done
40 Do one thing at a time

41 Always have something to do: even if it is constructive relaxation
42 Always be on time yourself
43 Handle paper only once if at all possible
44 Read only what you must: the rest can be read in your C time

TRAVELLING
45 Do not leave it until the last minute to set off
46 Do not be a one-side-of-the-town-to-the-other traveller: plan groups of visits within easy range of each other
47 Use car cassette learning
48 Consider having a car phone – outward calls only?
49 Use train time to: read, write, brainstorm ideas with yourself

SUMMARY
50 Plan *what* you have to do, *how* it is going to be done, *where* it is to be done, by *when* it has to be done. Why has it to be done at all?

From 'Training and Development' April 1988,
in an article by Leslie Rae FITD, p. 40

Consider this checklist against the prime purpose of this section, 'Can you sell it?' If a sensible use of this checklist creates more selling time for you, then you will be getting your priorities right.

Everything you do should contribute to your self improvement and thereby the improvement of your business. So use this checklist at regular intervals to review your progress and assess how much you have achieved – you will probably be pleasantly surprised.

Energy and health
The show must go on, or so the theatrical profession would have us believe. The show certainly must go on as far as a small business is concerned, especially for the sole trader, since there is no one else to 'perform'.

In setting up a new business, the energy and health of the participants is something which should receive serious consideration, since a lot of energy is going to be needed in those all-important early stages.

For example, if prior to setting up your own business you received as part of your employment package, an annual health check up, it is well worth considering continuing with this. Ask yourself whether you can afford to be ill in your new business situation, and that whether the fee for an annual checkup is a worthwhile expense, not to say investment in the most valuable asset your business has – you and your health.

There are many ways in which this can be done. It is worthwhile sorting out your arrangements at this early stage, before the pressures begin taking their toll.

If you are going to be selling your goods or services face to face with your prospective customers, you will need to be well on top of the task. In order to be alert and able to respond to the situation of the moment, you will need to have at least reasonable health.

You will find a lot of this initial activity both physically and mentally taxing, and you will need to be able to start each new day with a certain amount of zeal and enthusiasm. Even if you have been used to doing this sort of work before, the pressure of having your name 'over the door' adds an extra incentive to – and drain on – your energy resources.

Communication skills
In order to sell something, whether it is a product or a service, a certain degree of skill in communication is required. The actual process of selling is covered in detail in Chapter 6, but there are other methods of communication which are relevant in business.

SPOKEN
Spoken communication does not only apply to the selling situation, but is necessary for discussions with all sorts of people – potential customers, suppliers, reps, professional advisers, etc. These can be either face-to-face or via the telephone. The ability to be fluent and comprehensible, particularly on the telephone, is a skill to be developed.

One way of doing this is to record yourself on tape – if possible doing a real telephone call. When listening to it afterwards, do not think in general terms of how good and bad it is, but try to analyse:

- whether all the words can be clearly heard
- whether you say a lot of 'ums' and 'ers'
- whether you repeat yourself too much

- whether your voice sounds pleasant and friendly (try smiling down the phone)

You need not be afraid of recording the other person, because that voice will not be heard on your tape.

WRITTEN

Written communication is necessary in a number of areas – letters, estimates, quotations, invoices, etc. Your business communications must go out without spelling, grammar and punctuation mistakes. If you know you are weak in this area, use the services of someone who knows what they are doing. You will probably not have the time at this stage to improve your own English language skills. If you only need to brush up on your written English, try *English Language Skills* by Vera Hughes, published by Macmillan. Presentation of written communication is almost as important as the content, because the way written material is laid out reflects your business image. This is covered in Chapter 10.

Pilot scheme

Before committing yourself too deeply to your prospective business, it is quite a good idea to 'test the water'. If it is possible, compile a sample lot of your product, and embark on a selling exercise to test the reaction of potential buyers or outlets.

Try to gather as much useful information as possible during this exercise – pluses and minuses, assessing the strengths and weaknesses of what you have to offer, and the way in which you are presenting it.

To do this exercise when you are offering a service is a little more difficult, since what you have to offer is not as tangible as an actual product. Perhaps you could offer to provide a sample of your service at a very advantageous price in order to test the response of potential clients. The 'Marketing your Consultancy' section of Chapter 5 might be helpful to you in this situation.

Getting your business off the ground will often take a lot longer than you thought. There is a great deal to do in the early stages, and sometimes there are delays beyond your control. To minimise delay, invest time at these very early stages in learning how to do the research, the marketing and the selling in the most time- and cost-effective way.

CHAPTER 1 CHECKLIST

1 Make a list of the reasons why people should want to buy your product or service
2 Carry out some market research – seek help from your local Enterprise Agency and/or college
3 Make a list of potential suppliers and their strong points
4 Rate yourself on a 1–10 scale for the following:
   - Motivation
   - Organisational ability
   - Management of time
   - Fitness
   - Communication skills

   Decide what needs improving, and plan how to improve it
5 Run a pilot scheme

2

Money

In this Chapter

Costing the product or service *Cost price*; *Mark up and margin*; *Selling price*

Working Capital and Cash Flow

Making a Business Plan

Presenting your case for funding

Costing the product or service

Cost price

The costs of a business can be sub-divided into several categories, which will have an effect on arriving at the cost price of the product or service, either directly or indirectly.

Examples of costs are:

Labour
Direct workers: those directly involved in handling goods
Indirect workers: administration, support services, maintenance
In the small business one person could well be involved in both categories.

Machinery and materials
Components: goods and machines used to produce the finished product

Interest	Charges on borrowings: loans e.g. overdrafts
Overheads	Light, heat, rent, rates, telephone, travelling, postage, etc.
Taxes	National Insurance, VAT, Inland Revenue, etc.

Portions of these various costs need to be taken into account when arriving at the cost price of your product.

The same should be done if you are offering a service. What you are selling is your time, and you have to work out the value of that, while taking account of the costs of the business.

Mark up and margin

A business exists to make a profit; *your* business will exist only if it makes a profit. This profit is generally expressed in one of two ways – either as a percentage of the cost price or the selling price.

If based on the cost price it is referred to as **Mark Up**, and can be expressed as follows:

$$\frac{\text{Selling Price} - \text{Cost Price}}{\text{Cost Price}} \times 100$$

An example calculation:

$$\frac{£20.00 - £15.00}{£15.00} = \frac{5}{15} \times 100$$

$$= \frac{500}{15} = 33\tfrac{1}{3}\%$$

If based on the selling price it is referred to as **Margin**, and can be expressed as follows:

$$\frac{\text{Selling Price} - \text{Cost Price}}{\text{Selling Price}} \times 100$$

An example calculation:

$$\frac{£20.00 - £15.00}{£20.00} = \frac{5}{20} \times 100$$

$$= \frac{500}{20} = 25\%$$

Mark Up is always greater (in percentage terms) than Margin, although the monetary figure is the same. It is vital, if discussing

profit percentages, to establish whether the figures being quoted are Mark Up or Margin – confusion can follow if this is not done.

Mark Up and Margins can very easily be worked out on a calculator with a %️ key, probably along these lines:

Mark Up   SP – CP
               Answer ÷ CP
               %️ key = x%

Margin   SP – CP
               Answer ÷ SP
               %️ key = x%

Selling price
The selling price should provide a suitable margin between that and the cost price to produce a profit for the business. It must also reflect the market in which you trade. Find out what other people charge for a similar product or service. The profit must be adequate and continuous, and cover current expenses, while providing a balance for the future.

Working Capital and Cash Flow

Working Capital is the value of the current assets of the business *less* the current liabilities.

Assets	are what the business owns, and divide into two broad categories:
	Fixed assets – land and buildings, machinery, motor vehicles, etc.
	Current assets – debtors, stock, cash in hand, cash at bank, etc.
Liabilities	are what is owed to others, again divided into two broad categories:
	Long-term liabilities – capital introduced, bank loans, etc.
	Current liabilities – creditors, overdraft, wages and salaries, etc.

A business should never allow itself to run short of Working Capital, which should always be sufficient to finance the running of the business. Lack of Working Capital is a very common reason for business failure: it means, for example, that creditors cannot be paid, or advantage taken of special offers from suppliers. Working Capital ratio can be calculated as follows:

$$\frac{\text{Current Assets}}{\text{Current Liabilities}}$$

Although the ratio of 1:1 is the minimum Working Capital ratio, a business should endeavour to improve on this, and doing the calculation from time to time is a useful exercise. A business needs cash to be profitable, and has to ensure that the flow of cash does not dry up.

The obtaining of a large order seems good news to a small business, but care must be taken that the extra expense involved, particularly that of obtaining the materials necessary to fulfill the work, does not reduce the available cash to an unacceptable level – remember that the overheads and other fixed expenses still have to be met.

How can a business ensure that a sudden need for cash does not become a burden? One way is to try to keep abreast of the current financial situation. A bank statement will give an indication, albeit in hindsight, although a visit to the cash dispenser at the bank will give you the real up-to-date position. Beware, though, of acting on the figure displayed by the cash dispenser, because there might be some cheques which are as yet uncleared, or some regular payments which have not yet been deducted from the balance.

A method of establishing this on a more formalised basis is to draw up a Cash Flow Forecast, which will enable you to keep the up-to-date position constantly before you, and help you make the right decision when the unexpected turns up.

A Cash Flow Forecast should be drawn up for a twelve month period, although it could be done for a month or a quarter. Each month should show the Budget figures with space next to them for the Actual figures to be inserted. Here is a rough pattern (opposite):

Take appropriate action when A–B Balance varies from the Budget figure. Keep new work within the cash resources available.

CASH FLOW FORECAST				
Month	January		February	
	BUDGET	ACTUAL	BUDGET	ACTU/
Opening balance	—		—	
INCOMING				
– Sales				
– Debtors				
– Other				
A Total receipts				
OUTGOING				
– Materials				
– Creditors				
– Light/Heat				
– Rent/Rates				
– Wages/Salaries				
– Telephone/Postage etc.				
B Total payments				
A–B Balance (+ or –)				
CLOSING BALANCE (Transferred to next month)				

Turn down work if necessary to prevent Cash Flow problems – remember that a sale does not necessarily mean immediate payment; allow for delays in getting your money.

Make certain that the business never owes more than can be met by the current balance plus, if necessary, the value of any assets which could be sold. Try to show a sensible and realistic projected profit – one that is not too high or too low for your type of business.

Making a business plan

Producing a Business Plan will not automatically ensure that your business will be successful, but it will help you to face the future in a realistic way and, very important, present your business ideas to somebody else in a formal and factual manner.

The way in which the plan is drawn up and presented is important. The business which takes the trouble to produce its Business Plan in a logical and presentable way is more than likely to adopt the same approach to its business opportunities.

Visit the major banks and collect their booklets on Business Planning. You will find many helpful suggestions on how to draw up a Business Plan. It might be a wise move to base yours on the format suggested by the bank you intend to approach with your Business Plan!

Do not be afraid to seek assistance in drawing up your Business Plan, but beware of copying other people's. Your plan concerns your business and your business alone; your accountant can provide invaluable help in this task. It is not a job to be rushed; careful preparation stands a better chance of success than a document hurriedly thrown together. In any case keep it simple and to the point.

The headings you could consider for your Business Plan are:

Purpose of business	what you are going to sell and, broadly, in what sort of market
Marketing strategy	based on market research and carefully costed
Competition	where you fit in and where you differ
Starting up requirements	premises, machinery, materials, furniture, vehicles, telecommunications etc
Grey areas of the business	the unknown, points where you cannot yet be precise
The way forward	some idea of how long it will take to get your business really up and running

End on an optimistic and enthusiastic note.

Presenting your case for funding

Banks

Banks want to lend you money: it is a vital part of their business, but, of course, they want to be certain that your business is a suitable one with which to be involved.

It is worth doing a little research before approaching a bank. Do not just go to your local branch because it is the nearest. Banks tend to specialise in different areas; find out from people in a similar business which banks are likely to look favourably on your business.

For example, if you are setting up a business in the entertainment industry, you might stand the chance of getting a more sympathetic hearing if you took your Business Plan for producing a series of promotional videos to a bank in the West End of London rather than one in the West Country, because the London bank would be more used to dealing with that type of business, and would appreciate the nature of the risks involved.

A preliminary chat to see whether a bank is prepared to lend money to you at all is a good idea, and may save you time. If the answer is definitely 'No', you know where you stand.

When you have obtained your appointment, make sure you have everything ready. You need a well-presented Business Plan and Cash Flow Forecast.

Draw up a detailed list of:

* what you want the money for
* how you intend to pay it back

Remember to include the interest on the loan in your calculations.

It is better to ask for a long-term loan, so try to get as long a pay-back period as you can. It is always possible to pay back a loan early, but not always so easy to extend the loan if your business is not doing as well as you hoped.

Try to anticipate the questions you are likely to be asked. It would probably be sensible to arrange for your accountant to attend with you. In any case try to have a 'dry run' where you can state the main facts of your case and reassure yourself that you can do this with confidence.

Other sources of funding

Banks are not the only lenders of money, but a bank is a good start for up to £15,000. Above that figure you could consider a building society, an insurance company or a merchant bank. You could also consider topping up your mortgage to introduce capital into your business. Ask your accountant to advise you on sources of funding, where to go for the best deal and how best to present your request for a loan.

CHAPTER 2 CHECKLIST

1 How much will it cost to produce your product?
   or
   How much will it cost to render your service (including your time)?
2 What sort of profit margin will you expect to get?
3 What will be the selling price of your product or service?
4 How will you ensure that you have enough working capital and cashflow?
5 Have you done your Cash Flow Forecast?
6 Have you done your Business Plan?
7 If you need funding, have you detailed what you need and how you are going to pay it back?

3

Premises

In this Chapter

Working from home

Workshops, warehouses and
  factories

Office premises

Finding out what is available

Support and grants

NB for retail outlets see
Chapter 12

Working from home

For some people, working from home is out of the question,
because of manufacturing processes, storage space required, for
instance, but for many it can be a good starting point. The types of
business which are suitable for working from home are likely to be:

- Consultancy
- Teaching/training
- 'Cottage' industry (e.g. crafts, food)
- Professions (e.g. accountants, therapists, architects)

Sometimes a good business address is essential to your image; in this
case an obviously residential address would be a handicap.

Customer and client access

If yours is the type of business where you go to your clients or
customers – goods made at home and delivered or services rendered
on other people's premises perhaps – a home base could work quite
well.

It is essential that your customers are able to get in touch with you quickly and easily, by phone, fax or computer at times convenient to them. You also have to guard your own privacy, however, and make it clear that business is to be done in business hours, whatever those may be. For example, if your business hours exclude mornings, and you work afternoons, evenings and weekends, this must be made clear to your customers. Home hairdressing could be an example here.

If your business requires your customers to come to you, if only occasionally (consultants or accountants, for instance), it is very important to be able to receive them in a business-like atmosphere, with all the privacy they would expect from business premises. Parking should be convenient, if possible, and the entry to your home easy and pleasant. Being greeted by a doorbell which does not work, a barking dog and a noisy child is not a good introduction to a business atmosphere.

If you are doing business with customers in your home, a separate office or study is highly desirable.

Space
If your business is a cottage industry, you obviously need enough space in which to process what you are making. A shed or garage can sometimes be used. Remember that you will also need storage space for:

- equipment
- materials, including wrapping or packing materials
- tools
- items ready for delivery to customers

and good access for getting these things in and out of your home without causing annoyance to the rest of your household or your neighbours.

You will also need space for the office side of the business (see Chapter 10). Equipment such as fax machines, photocopiers and typewriters or personal computers takes up quite a bit of room, and is often difficult to move because of size or access to power points. A separate office is ideal, if possible. Remember that you will need a phone in the 'office' as well as where you are working.

If you are supplying a service, as opposed to a product, from your home, less space is needed, but you still need to be able to store paper, files, office machinery and so on. Take account of this, and try to keep your business space and your private space separate.

Routine
It is important to set yourself some sort of routine for working from home. You do not have the discipline of leaving for another place of work, and it is very easy to get sidetracked.

Working from home means that you do not spend time travelling to work, but you have to be strict about the time you therefore save. If you decide to set this time aside for personal matters, that is your decision and one of the benefits of being self-employed and working from home.

It is easy to get distracted by:

- external noises (lawn mower, traffic)
- internal noises (animals, children, TV, radio)

It is also easy to be interrupted by:

- callers (meter reader, delivery vans)
- visitors
- family and friends
- personal phone calls
- domestic chores (cooking, cleaning, shopping, fetching children from school, etc.)

People tend to think that because you are at home you are not working. If you can establish a routine for your work it will help your own discipline and that of other people. You need to come to an agreement with other members of the household about who does what, when and where. If you have been used to working in an office or a factory, you will find it quite difficult to adapt to the routine of working at or from home, and you should make allowances for this adjustment period.

Overheads
You need to be clear, as soon as possible, what proportion of the overheads on your home you can claim for business purposes. You should be able to claim a proportion of your:

- lighting and heating
- telephone
- security
- cleaning

} if necessary

Reckon on being able to claim anything to do with the business, not with the house. If you start claiming for rates or water rates, you may be liable to Capital Gains Tax when you sell the house. The Community Charge (Poll Tax) should not be affected at all by the fact that you work from home.

Check with your accountant what proportion of household expenses can be deemed to be for business use and how this should be recorded in the books (see Chapter 7). For example, you should be able to claim VAT (if you are VAT registered) on your business telephone calls, and on a proportion of any telephone rental charges, provided you do not already claim for rates.

If you have cleaning help in the home some of this payment might be offset as a business expense, but take care that your cleaning person does not become an employee for personal tax or NI purposes.

Other things you might be able to claim for are a guard dog, installing security devices, extra telephone points and secretarial services by other members of the household, but check with your accountant first.

You need to be sure, when setting up your business at home, that you are not altering the use of the property or part of it from residential to light industrial. Check with the local authority bye-laws and a solicitor who is fully conversant with these.

Advantages and disadvantages of working from home

Advantages
- cheaper
- no travelling
- can help with domestic finances
- flexibility

Disadvantages
- distractions and interruptions
- lack of space
- lack of business address
- lack of business atmosphere

Workshops, warehouses and factories

If you are dealing with products, as opposed to services, you will often need to rent premises in which to work. Premises available can range from small workshops of no more than 500 sq. ft to small factories, depending on requirements. It is unusual for someone starting out in business to need a large factory straight away, but it is possible.

A warehouse is normally used for storage purposes only – storage of materials before processing, storage of deliveries ready for despatch or storage if you are the middleman between the seller and the buyer.

SIZE

The size depends on what you are producing, the size of the machinery or equipment you use and the amount of space needed for immediate storage of materials, packaging, wrapping and the finished product ready for despatch. It is sometimes more cost-effective to rent a slightly larger workshop which will accommodate all these requirements comfortably than to rent a separate storage area or warehouse.

When calculating the size required, remember to allow adequate space for the people who are going to work there, for facilities for those people (personal belongings storage, refreshments and so on) and for a certain amount of office space. Even if you are doing the books elsewhere (at home, for example) you will need a space on site for processing paperwork; this space might need to house a small computer. You will certainly need somewhere to put the phone.

ACCESS

You need easy access to your premises for:

- yourself
- your staff
- deliveries
- despatch

Make sure that you can get in to your premises when you want to – 24 hours if necessary. Make sure that your staff can get in if you are not there for any reason.

Consider access for large delivery vehicles, particularly if you buy in bulk. What unloading facilities are there?

Is there adequate parking for you, your staff and your own

vehicle(s) for despatching goods? What are the loading facilities for your own vehicles? Are lifts available if necessary?

Try making a list of all the people and products which will be going in and out of the premises and check for each whether they can get in and out in a cost-effective and practical way.

SECURITY

What security measures are in force to protect the premises you are going to rent? If you have 24-hour access, who else does? How secure are the windows and doors? How secure will your merchandise or products be while being unloaded and loaded? What lighting arrangements are there? What security system will you be allowed to install, if you need to? What security arrangements can be made for personal belongings?

Check the security:

- outside the premises
- inside the premises
- when receiving deliveries
- when despatching deliveries
- of personal property and vehicles
- of company vehicles

HEALTH AND SAFETY

Make sure you are aware of the provisions of the Health and Safety at Work Act 1974 (HASAWA). Check:

- environment (toxic substances, perhaps)
- machine guards and rules and regulations for cleaning and maintenance
- fire exits
- fire appliances
- evacuation procedures
- protective clothing, if necessary

If you are an employer, you are responsible for providing safe and healthy working conditions for your staff (see Chapter 11).

If your workshop, factory or warehouse is part of an industrial complex, you need to check the health and safety regulations relating to that complex, and that you are able to comply with them.

Remember to check the safety of your company vehicles and to have them regularly serviced, particularly if they are driven by someone other than yourself.

COST
It is impossible to suggest a fair rent for premises because this varies so widely in different parts of the country, and often in different parts of the same town.

It is helpful to make a list of what is *essential* to you when searching for premises and what is *desirable*. Also, considering your Cash Flow Forecast (see Chapter 2, page 14), set a maximum rent you are prepared to pay, and stick to it. Remember you might have to pay a one-off premium, sometimes returnable at the termination of the tenancy, as well as rent in advance when you agree to rent the premises.

Check whether the rent quoted is inclusive or exclusive of such items as rates, communal services (night watchman, window cleaning, for instance), building maintenance and so on. Are there any hidden extras?

It is not always the cheapest rent which is the most economical. Balance your *needs* against your preferences; if the property does not meet the essentials you require, go elsewhere: be prepared to pay a bit more if necessary, but not beyond the maximum you have set yourself.

Office premises

If you are offering a service, it might not be appropriate to work from home because of lack of space. Perhaps you are in partnership, and it would not be sensible to work from the home of either or any of the partners. In these cases you will be looking for office accommodation to rent.

Much of what was said under *Workshops, warehouses and factories* applies here. You need to consider:

- what size you need
- access to your office
- security
- health and safety and
- cost

There are, however, additional matters to be considered when renting office accommodation.

IMAGE

A good address and prestigious offices are vital to some businesses. For example, an interior design consultancy needs an address and office premises and furniture in keeping with its up-market image. It is worth looking in areas which are being gentrified as well as those which are well established as prestige areas. If you can get in early in an area which is about to move up-market, so much the better.

Again it will depend on whether clients come to you or you go to them, but it is unusual for your offices never to be visited by potential clients, whatever your business. Therefore you need offices into which you will not be ashamed to welcome visitors, without going into unnecessary expense. This is tied up with the next section on Services.

SERVICES

Sometimes office accommodation comes with certain services, such as cleaning, window cleaning, reception, switchboard, fax, telex, mail in and out. You should check which of these services is included in the rent, if any.

When visiting the premises, if it is an office block of which you intend to rent one small part, note how well the reception area is maintained, whether the grass (if any) is cut, whether the plants are tended and how well you are received by the Receptionist. These are all indicative of how well the building is run and this is an indication of the image that will be conveyed to your own clients.

If you are planning to rent premises above shops, visit during the busiest time of the day so that you can judge the noise levels or smells from neighbouring premises to see whether they are acceptable.

ACCOMMODATION

When calculating the square footage of accommodation you require, remember to take account of the provisions of the Offices, Shops and Railway Premises Act, which lays down, among other things, how much working space each person should have, and what toilet facilities should be available.

Look for adequate power points for your office machinery and desk lamps, and check that the temperature can be regulated so that it is not too cold for the people nor too hot for the equipment.

Office workers normally require either good car parking facilities or easy access to shops and public transport.

Finding out what is available

The main sources of information about what is available in the way of business premises to rent are:

- Estate agents who specialise in that type of property
- Local authorities, for premises owned and rented by them
- Your local library
- Local Enterprise Agencies
- Your own observations

Libraries

If your local library is a good one – that is, it offers an up-to-date reference section and knowledgeable staff – you have a highly-prized source of information. It can supply you with copies of:

- Specialist books on finding premises
  (e.g. *A Shop of Your Own*; *Estate Agents*, Kogan Page publications)
- Lists of professional advisers
- Lists of premises available
- Publications on how to choose and rent premises
- The Land Registers which show publicly-owned land which is underutilised
- The Business Location Handbook by area in the UK
- Enterprise Zones, planning offices etc.

Estate agents

The library will probably have a list of agents which specialise in business premises. Local business directories are helpful.

An agent with local knowledge is an advantage. Test by asking about a property of which you have personal knowledge to see what the agent has to say about it.

Local enterprise agencies

These are Agencies set up by the government, and are normally sponsored by big firms locally. As well as offering free advice to new businesses, they often have premises which they can let at a very reasonable rent. These premises are usually workshops to get you started; you are therefore encouraged to find other premises after about a year.

Conditions vary, because LEAs are autonomous, but it is worth seeking their help to find suitable premises. They are not themselves professional estate agents, bankers or solicitors, but they can advise you where to go next.

Local authorities

Local authorities often own large areas of property and are prepared to rent office and manufacturing accommodation to small businesses. They also hold records of planning applications, so that you can look up where developments are likely to occur and therefore where premises are likely to be available. They will also have details of Enterprise Parks and industrial estates. The local telephone directory will normally give some indication of the correct department to approach.

Your own observation

Keep a look-out yourself for likely empty premises. Look above shops and in basements, particularly for office accommodation. Nearby shops and offices will often know who the landlord is.

Watch for signs of private and public developments – premises gutted, new access roads being built. A property which is being run down might be a good short-term bet for you, because terms are likely to be favourable.

Support and grants

This section is about government and local authority support for renting premises. It is difficult to be precise about this, because government policy changes and the funds available from local authorities fluctuate.

As a rule of thumb, areas which government and local authorities want to promote, such as areas of high unemployment or deserted factories, are more likely than areas which are booming to offer support to growing businesses. Such areas might be termed Enterprise Zones or Development Areas.

Support is more likely to come in the form of subsidies for premises to rent than as direct grants, although grants are sometimes available for setting up specific projects – new technology, for example. These grants tend to go to the larger enterprises, but if you are embarking on a business which is either in the right geographical area or of the right type, it is worth making enquiries. The DTI (Department of Trade and Industry) has the information.

CHAPTER 3 CHECKLIST
1 Make a list of what is *essential* and what is desirable
2 Decide whether to work from home or not
3 When renting workshop, warehouse, factory or office accommodation consider:
 ● Size
 ● Access
 ● Security
 ● Health and Safety
 ● Image
 ● Services
 ● Cost: set a maximum you can afford, and stick to it

4 To find out what is available use:
 ● Local authorities
 ● Estate agents
 ● Libraries
 ● Local Enterprise Agencies
 ● Your own observation

5 For government and local authority support, consult:
 ● Department of Trade and Industry (Tel: 071 215 7877)
 ● Local authority (number in The phone Book)

4

Methods of Trading

In this Chapter

Sole trader

Partnership

Limited company

Franchise

Co-operative

Registered charity

Multi-level marketing

Sole trader

If you are a one-person business, perhaps working from home, probably the best method of trading is as a sole trader. You do not need to register with any official body, but you do need some stationery with your name and business address (see Chapter 10). You need to inform the Inland Revenue and the DSS that you are self-employed and if your *turnover* (that is, the amount of money you actually take in sales in a financial year) is £23,500 or more (1989 figures) you need to be VAT registered (see Chapter 7 and Chapter 9). It is surprising how quickly your turnover will reach this figure.

If you are trading under your own name – for instance, 'John Robinson Associates', or 'J. Robinson' or something very similar – you do not need to check whether someone else is trading under the same name. If you choose to trade under a name which is quite different from yours (for example, 'Parisian Photos'), check with your solicitor that there are no legal objections to your doing so. Your own name and address must still appear on your stationery.

As a sole trader you are personally responsible for all your business transactions. This means that your personal income, from whatever source, your house, your car and even your estate after your death can be used to pay off debts. Some people make sure that the house is at least in joint names and that other possessions (such as the car) are registered in the name of another member of the family. Check with your solicitor the best way of covering yourself. You do not have to have your accounts audited, but it is as well to employ an accountant who specialises in very small businesses to prepare your annual accounts and tax returns for Inland Revenue purposes (see Chapter 9).

Partnership

If two or more of you are working together in the business, you can trade as a partnership. Like a sole trader, you do not have to register your business, but you do have to:

- Show your names and address on your stationery
- Inform the Inland Revenue and the DSS that you are self-employed
- Check that any name under which you choose to trade is legally acceptable
- Register for VAT if your turnover exceeds £23,500 per year (1989 figures)

All the Partners are collectively and individually liable for the debts of the business. This includes any business debts of any of the partners, even if you do not know that these debts have been incurred.

You are not required by law to draw up a Partnership Agreement, but it is wise to do this, setting out all the conditions under which you have agreed to enter into business together. A solicitor specialising in small businesses and partnerships will be able to advise you.

The partnership ceases instantly upon the death of any of the partners, so it is wise to take out life insurance on each partner so that the remaining partner(s) have enough money to continue trading if they want to. The deceased partner's share of the business becomes part of his or her personal estate.

As with a sole trader, you do not have to have your accounts audited, but it is wise to employ an accountant for Inland Revenue purposes.

Limited company

Many small businesses choose to set themselves up as a limited company. The big advantage of this method of trading is that your business liability is limited to the business, and you would not be required to pay debts out of your personal moneys, except in the case of fraud.

A limited company must have a minimum of two shareholders who act as director and company secretary, and the company must be registered with the Companies Registration Office (CRO), Companies House, Crown Way, Maindy, Cardiff.

The Company's stationery must show its name and address and place and number of registration. The fact that it is 'limited' must appear somewhere on the paper – either in the company name or as a separate statement. The stationery must also show the names (first name or initials plus surname) of either all the directors or none of them.

The accounts must be properly audited by a qualified accountant within 9 months of the end of the company's financial year and filed annually at the CRO, so that anyone, particularly shareholders who are not Directors of the company, can inspect them if they wish. A qualified accountant will have FCA, FAPA or ACCA after his or her name. The accountant is usually appointed at the first Annual General Meeting and continues as auditor as long as both parties wish.

You raise capital by selling shares in the company to the Directors and others. The Chairman of the company, if one is appointed, is normally responsible to the shareholders.

The outline of the company's trading purposes and methods is drawn up in the Memorandum and Articles of Association (often known as Mem and Arts). The Memorandum outlines the purpose of the company (its overall strategy) and the Articles of Association outline the way in which it will work – number of Directors, voting rights and so on – (the company tactics). These documents need to be drawn up carefully; you should employ a solicitor.

You can buy a ready-made limited company 'off-the-shelf' from a company registration agent, with its Mem and Arts already prepared; virtually all you need to do is fill in the names of the Director(s) and Secretary and the company's proposed address, and pay the appropriate fee. You need to be sure that any such business meets your own requirements.

You can, of course, buy a business which already exists, including its goodwill, so that you can start trading straight away. In this case you need to look very carefully at its accounts, because they can be deceptive (without any intention to deceive). Employ an accountant for this; it is false economy not to do so.

Franchise

This is becoming a very popular way of starting up in business, and can be a sensible way of doing so, because you can profit from the know-how of the Franchisor (you would be the Franchisee). Some very well-known companies run a franchise – household names like Body Shop, Prontaprint, Wimpy, and Thorntons, to name a few.

The *advantages* of becoming a franchisee are:

- You are trading under a well-known name
- You receive advice and training in, for example, merchandising, stock control, buying, employing staff, book-keeping, etc.
- Franchisors often have a special arrangement with a bank for getting start-up money (see Chapter 2).
- You are part of nationwide advertising
- Sometimes the Franchisor will find suitable premises and will lease or mortgage the premises to the Franchisee

Disadvantages are:

- You have to pay a franchise fee
- You would have to pay an ongoing management fee – perhaps 10% of the turnover
- The start-up capital can be quite large – up to £500,000 – but can be as low as £5,000
- You have to stick to the systems laid down by the Franchisor so freedom to trade in the manner in which you wish to trade can be a little limited

There are two main types of franchise for the small business:

- Retailing in a wide variety of fashionable shops and eating establishments: income depends on the profits made
- Rendering a service, such as carpet cleaning or car tuning: income often depends on the number of hours worked

More information about franchising can be obtained from The British Franchise Association, 75a Bell Street, Henley-on-Thames, Oxon RG9 2BD.

Co-operatives

This is a business which is jointly owned by its members – a minimum of seven people. Setting up a co-operative is not a simple operation, and you should seek advice from the National Co-operative Development Agency, Broadmead House, 21 Panton Street, London SW1 4DR. A co-operative has to be registered under the Industrial and Provident Societies Acts.

Registered Charities

For some businesses such as theatre companies, church organisations and people connected with the performing arts, it is possible to be incorporated as a registered charity.

The advantages of being a registered charity are, in 1989,

- 50% **rates** relief for buildings or land occupied by a charity or used wholly or mainly for charitable purposes. You will need to check the position as regards the Community Charge from 1990.
- Exemptions from **Income Tax** arising under Schedules A–D and F, if the income is applied for charitable purposes only.
- Profits of a trade carried on by a charity are exempt from Schedule D Income Tax if the profits are applied solely for the purpose of a charity and
  either the trade is exercised in the course of actually carrying out of the primary purpose of the charity
  or the work in connection with the trade is mainly carried out by beneficiaries of a charity.

- Exemptions from **Corporation Tax** in the same way.
- No **Capital Gains Tax** chargeable on gifts to charities or payable by charities.
- Lifetime gifts and gifts in a will or settlement are exempt from **Inheritance Tax**.

As you can see, the tax advantages can be quite considerable, but the rules governing charities are strict. A company which tries to squeeze itself into a 'charitable' mould when it is really not a charity will find it harder to obey the rules.

The general rules are these:

1   The charity unit must be registered with the Charity Commissioners, and the purpose of the charity must be charitable.

The definition of 'charitable' is not clear cut, but falls mainly within one of four categories and must be for the public benefit. The categories are:
- relief of poverty
- advancement of education
- advancement of religion
- other purpose beneficial to the community

2   The trustees of the charity may not profit from their position as trustees (but they may receive remuneration for their work within the charity).

3   The trustees must inform the Charity Commissioners of certain changes.

4   The trustees must keep the accounts.

5   Where the charity is a Company Limited by Guarantee (which is often the case with, for example, a theatre company), the objects of the company must be acceptable to the Charity Commissioners.

It is a fairly complicated matter to register as a charity. You should seek advice from your solicitor, or, in the case of theatre companies, write to Interchange, 15 Wilkin Street, London NW5 3NG. A very helpful booklet is published by the Scottish Arts Council called *Care, Diligence and Skill*. It does not deal exclusively with registered charities but is an excellent *Handbook for the Governing Bodies of Arts Organisations*, which is its sub-title.

Multi-level marketing

This is a very specialised method of trading. It is often advertised by alluring advertisements in the Sunday papers which invite you to 'EARN £££s WORKING FROM HOME' or 'INVEST IN THE BUSINESS OFFER OF A LIFETIME'. Multi-level marketing is not illegal, and can make quite substantial income for those who wish to employ this trading method. It is a respectable development from pyramid selling, which got itself a bad name in the 1960's.

How does it work?

You join a trading scheme as a 'participant' and buy goods or services from the person or people running the scheme, or from other participants. You then sell these goods or services to the general public in their homes.

You make a profit on the difference between the the cost (buying) price and the selling price and usually by other rewards such as:

• bonuses for recruiting new participants
• commission on sales of your products made by other participants
• higher bonuses or commission if you are promoted to a higher level in the scheme
• payments for providing services (e.g. training) to other participants

You need to be good at selling things and/or recruiting other participants if you are to make a substantial income from this type of scheme.

There are very strict rules laid down under Part XI of the Fair Trading Act 1973 and the Pyramid Selling Schemes Regulations 1973. There is a helpful leaflet about Pyramid Selling Schemes published by the Department of Trade and Industry Consumer Affairs Division 3, Room 411, 10–18 Victoria Street, London SW1H 0NN.

Multi-level marketing can be a profitable way of doing business, but you need to beware of illegal schemes, or getting caught up in a legal scheme without fully realising its implications.

CHAPTER **4** CHECKLIST

1 Sole Trader:
- One-person business
- No registration requirement
- Headed stationery
- Inform Inland Revenue and DSS
- Personally liable

2 Partnership:
- Two or more partners
- No registration required
- Headed stationery
- All partners liable for debts
- Partnership ceases on death of one of them
- Partnership Agreement desirable

3 Limited Company
- Liability limited to the business
- Must register with Companies Registration Office (Tel: 0222 388588)
- Accounts must be audited by qualified Accountant
- Minimum of two shareholders
- Headed stationery must show address, registration number and 'limited'. All directors' names or none
- Memorandum and Articles of Association required

4 Franchise
- Advantages: well-known name; advice and training; help with funding; sometimes help with premises
- Disadvantages: franchise fee; ongoing management fee; limited freedom in trading practice
- Information from The British Franchise Association (Tel: 0491 578049)

5 Co-operative
- Minimum of seven people
- Must be registered
- Seek advice from the National Co-operative Development Agency (Tel: 071 839 2988)

6 Registered charity
- Many tax advantages
- Strict rules to follow
- Must have charitable purposes
- Must negotiate with Charity Commissioners
- Suitable for arts organisations

7 Multi-level marketing
- Become a 'participant' in a scheme
- Buy from other participants
- Sell to other participants or general public
- Expected to recruit other participants
- Strict rules to follow
- Beware illegal schemes

5

Marketing

In this Chapter

Your marketing profile
Marketing methods
  Advertisements;
  Mailshots; Leaflet drops;
  Printing and artwork

  requirements; Leads and
  personal contacts
Marketing your own
  consultancy
Image

Your marketing profile

Having decided on the product or service your business is going to be offering, it is important to invest time in deciding how this product or service is going to be presented in the most effective way – your marketing profile.

Perhaps the tried and tested method of self question could be most appropriate in defining precisely what the business is all about. The actual answer will vary considerably, of course, depending on the type of business involved, but in general terms this could be a pattern to follow:

What are we selling?

• a product, a service, a skill

Who will be our customers?

• will they be regulars who will keep coming back to us
• will they be casual passers-by

- will they be trade, who will then sell on our product to others
- will they be the end users of our product

Who will be the actual buyer of our product or service?

- particularly in large organisations, who will be the decision-maker

What will our customers actually need?

- will our basic product/service be sufficient
- will there be opportunities for selling 'extras'

Where is our market?

- what is likely demand for what we are offering
- what is the size of the existing market
- what is our potential share likely to be
- what is likely to be the spending power of potential customers

What is the competition?

- how intense is the competition
- who are they
- how well do they meet the needs of their customers
- are there areas of weakness which provide opportunities for our business

From these generalities, try to draw up a precise self-questioning checklist for your business. A lot of wasted time and money, the possible result if a product or service is presented in a rather arbitrary way, can be avoided by such an analysis.

Marketing methods

You need to let people know that your business exists, what you have to offer and how your customers could benefit from using its products or services. This is the aim of marketing.

There are various methods of marketing which are available to a business. Some are more suitable than others, so part of the secret of successful marketing is using those methods which are likely to be the most effective.

Advertisements

Very broadly, advertisments – and advertising generally – can be divided into two categories, selective and non-selective.

With *selective* advertisements you will be aiming your material at particular groups or categories of potential customer, whom you have previously identified. This identification could well be one of the results of your self-questioning exercise under Presenting the Product or Service (see pages 39–40) – which makes the time spent on that task even more worthwhile.

One advantage of selective advertising is that you can be very precise in your material, perhaps even to the extent of incorporating a modest jargon word or two, since your target audience will understand. It might also create a (subconscious) impression on the readers that you know what you are talking about – which, of course, you do.

Non-selective advertising on the other hand, by its very nature, must be more general in its approach, striking a balance between being too basic or elementary for those in the know, and inviting the person who is unfamiliar with the subject matter to find out more.

This leads us neatly into the well-used advertising formula AIDA – which is particularly applicable to non-selective advertising, for what AIDA aims to do, through the advertising material, is to:

- Gain the **A**ttention of the reader
- Hold the **I**nterest of the reader
- Create a **D**esire in the reader for your product or service
- Stimulate **A**ction in the reader to B U Y

which, after all, is the sole purpose of advertisements. It is the route toward this target which needs careful planning.

Advertisements cost money: ineffective advertisements waste money. There are three main sources of expense involved in advertisements: firstly, the design and layout of your message; secondly, the actual production of the advertisement and finally the distribution of the advertisement.

DESIGN AND LAYOUT

Even if you undertake this yourself, remember your time is money, so there is still an expense involved. It could be worth your while enlisting the help of someone who is knowledgeable in copywriting and layout. At the very least study the advertisements of businesses promoting a similar product or service to yours. Compile a scrap-book for easy reference – this could help you devise a design and layout of your own. Remember what we said about the importance of image in advertising matter.

PRODUCTION

This includes the expense of the actual printing process, and everything which leads up to that moment, like setting up the text, and producing plates.

One very useful tip at this stage – *always* proofread any advertising material; if possible get someone else to do it as well. This can save a lot of heartache when an error is discovered after the print run is completed.

DISTRIBUTION

How distribution is carried out will depend on the form of the advertisement. If it is printed in a newspaper or magazine, the distribution will be controlled by the circulation of the publication.

If it is your business or service you are advertising, as distinct from the products, the advertisement will take a different form. Perhaps a display advertisement in a local paper or Yellow Pages or other local directory.

If you have a telephone line, or a group of lines rented from British Telecom at the business rate, you have a free entry in Yellow Pages under the available classification of your choice. This will consist of your name, address and telephone number in light print. However, it is possible to have various types of display advertising: information on these possibilities can be found by contacting Yellow Pages Sales Ltd – the number is in your Yellow Pages Directory.

Mailshots

Being on the receiving end of mailshots, one could be forgiven for thinking that they are the most effective form of advertising known to man, since everyone seems to use them. But consider for a moment how many you, personally, have responded to; probably only a very few. This is the big minus for this form of advertising – the response rate is traditionally low, and yet it remains a much used method. One incentive to advertisers, initially, might be the free mailshot offer which the Post Office makes to first-time users.

As with advertisements, mailshots can be selective or non-selective. Unless you intend to send mailshots in very large numbers, it would be advisable to use selective mailshots to specified target groups. This could be approached in several ways, for instance alphabetical, geographical. Try to compile as big a list as possible of organisations which might use your product or service. List the most obvious ones first, but do not be too rigid, particularly if you are offering products or services which have a more universal application. Think of organisations which, although they might be diverse in themselves, have a common need which is covered by your product or service. Ask yourself: how many products do I have and does this affect how many potential customers are available for my business?

When you have compiled your list, rather than tackle it all in one go, work though it piecemeal and select a manageable number: this will help you to regulate the time involved in preparation, follow up and evaluating the results. This does not mean to say that you only need to prepare the number of mailshots you actually plan to send out. If you have a period of time in which you can make up a large number of packs, by all means do so. You do not necessarily have to despatch them all at the same time.

As a rule of thumb, aim to send each mailshot to a named person. This may involve a telephone call to find out from a business who is responsible for your product or service.

Obtain:

- the name and job title
- correct name of the company
- the full postal address

You cannot always rely on Trade Directory information, even in the current edition, because people move, change jobs and businesses get taken over; it is best to check.

Write to the 'big boys' on your list first, even if you feel there is not much hope because they have everything tied up already. If this turns out to be the case, at least you know for sure, but there again at the particular time they may be in the market to consider your product or service . . .

The mailshot package itself will probably consist of a brochure or some other form of printed matter describing your product or service, together with a standard letter of introduction. Follow the KISS principle and Keep It Short and Simple. Do not be tempted to tell the recipients your whole story at this first encounter – but just enough for them to want to know more.

Try to keep your letter to one side of one sheet of headed paper – remember the importance of layout, which we considered under Image.

Follow this broad format: introduce yourself and your organisation by stating who you are and what you are offering, and in effect ask 'Can we do business?'. Indicate that you intend to follow up this written introduction with a telephone call.

In the letter, do not quote a precise time when you will ring (something may prevent you) or suggest a specific date for a meeting (you do not know the recipient's commitments), but wait until you telephone, when you will have a direct response to a suggested date, and alternatives can be discussed – and resolved – there and then.

Set yourself a deadline, and some sort of timetable for your telephone follow-up calls. Probably the best times, from the recipients' point of view, is Tuesday to Thursday, preferably mornings if you can make it. Monday mornings and Friday afternoons are probably best avoided – the recipients are just getting their week underway on the one, and thinking about going off on the other. There might well be cases, of course, where these *are* the ideal times to telephone. You will get to know your own type of business best.

Preparation for your follow-up telephone call will help it to be effective. Compile a checklist of points to make. Try to avoid a fully-written-out script. You can be thrown if the recipient does not respond in the way you expect – or asks a question at the wrong time!

Your call could take this form, once you are connected to the right person:

Identify yourself and your organisation.

Ask whether your brochure has been received, to which the answer will broadly be 'Yes' or 'No'.

If the answer is 'No', briefly explain the substance of your letter and brochure in broad terms (having a copy of both in front of you will prove invaluable in these circumstances).

Offer to send a further set.

At this stage, and if the answer to your original question was 'Yes', ask whether your kind of product or type of service is being stocked or used at present. Again the answer will broadly be 'Yes' or 'No'.

This is your cue to describe the benefits to that business of what you are offering; in the case of the 'No' answer you can start from basics, with the 'Yes' response, explain what is *different* about yours, and the benefits to that business of including your product or service in their existing range.

If at this stage there are discernible signs of interest, try to gain a definite commitment of some sort, e.g. a meeting, or even a sample order.

Be sure to confirm any arrangements in writing, and ensure that they are met in full.

If, however, the response is still negative, ask whether there is any possibility of reconsidering in the future, and whether you may ring again.

It might be worthwhile sending a letter thanking the individual for the conversation, and confirming that you will be in touch in a few months.

File the information for future reference – and mark your diary to remind you to make that call when the time comes around.

Leaflet drops

Leaflets can be a very reasonable way of passing on your message to potential customers, particularly if those customers are the end users, and leaflets can be distributed directly into their homes via their letterboxes. As with mailshots, one must accept that the take-up rate can be low.

This distribution could be done by hand, by post or even as inserts in special interest magazines.

The first method is obviously the cheapest. It is a job one could do oneself, or perhaps by cajoling members of the family into helping. Perhaps your friendly newsagent could be persuaded to allow the paperboys and girls to deliver your leaflets with (not in) the papers, to give a blanket, nonselective, coverage.

Post would involve more expense – remember the Post Office free first time offer, though. A wider geographical area could be covered, especially if you were doing a selective distribution and trying to target the right type of firm or household.

Inserting your leaflet into specialist publications could be another way of achieving a selective distribution – the cost might be comparable with that of a direct postal distribution, so could be worth looking into.

But what of the leaflet itself? Like the mailshot, there is only a short time to get your message across – between the letterbox and the waste bin! This means that the techniques you use in compiling your leaflet must gain the immediate attention of the recipient (AIDA applies in this situation, too), and be relevant to the product or service you want to sell – and do not forget, that is why you are doing the exercise.

Consider 'visual aids' to attract the attention of the person picking up your leaflet, and to underline your selling message. Drawings, photographs, cartoons could all come into this category – but choose with care, they must reflect the correct image of what you are offering.

Think about the actual material you will use for the leaflet: something suitable to the image, for instance plain paper or coloured paper? Glossy or matt finish? What sort of weight paper would be appropriate? Would thin card be going too far?

The size of the leaflet could be significant. Would A5 be too small or A4 too large? Will it be a flat sheet, or will it be folded? If so, how – in two or in three? (Who will do the folding and how long will it take? – what would be the extra cost, and would it be worthwhile?)

Give any prices you quote on the leaflet a 'life', for example, 'Valid until end of June' 'Special offer for July only' or indicate a time span by implication – 'Spring 1991'.

Make any follow-up action easy: prepaid reply, freephone, credit card payment.

Leaflet drops could be a cost-effective way of testing the market with a business idea. As with the mailshot method, take a conscious look at the leaflets which you receive through your door or in the post, and use them as a yardstick to designing an effective one of your own.

Printing and artwork requirements

Pretty well all the things we have been considering in this chapter could involve printing and artwork in varying degrees.

This is an area in which it is worth doing a little research. There are many, many printers about, as a glance in your Yellow Pages or free press will show you. You need to find those who specialise in the type of work you want. Perhaps the printer who produces your stationery is not the right one to produce your mailshot or advertising leaflet.

Very likely the printers who produce advertising material will have their own people or contacts to produce suitable artwork.

You will very often find the name of the printer on pieces of advertising material you receive from other people. If the standard or style is the sort of thing you are looking for, a visit or a phone call might be profitable.

Printing can be expensive, so try to get things cut and dried before committing yourself.

Leads and personal contacts

Personal contact can be a very valuable source of seeking business in the early days of trading, particularly among those who knew you in the business world before you set up your own enterprise. Your name and reputation will still mean something – this will fade, of course, with the passing of time, and as you build up an identity under your own name.

These personal contacts, if of no *direct* use to you, could be the means of pointing you towards others who could make use of your product or services. Utilise this method of introduction to the full in these critical early days, they could help you to establish a useful track record. Always have your business card handy to give to your personal contacts.

A word of thanks to the giver of a successful lead would no doubt be appreciated, and, who knows, others may be forthcoming!

Marketing your own consultancy

If you are selling a product, you have something tangible to show and demonstrate to prospective customers. If you are running a consultancy, the situation is somewhat different. In effect what you are selling is your time and your expertise. This means that the *quality* of any materials you produce, not only stationery and advertising, but the actual working documents, must be of the highest standard, both in content and presentation – these are, in fact, your product. Personal presentation must also reflect the standards of your consultancy.

Public Relations (PR) is an effective marketing technique; a means of keeping your consultancy in front of potential clients. Consider sending little snippets of information, or human interest anecdotes relating to you and your consultancy to your specialist publications, association newsletter, or even your local press. Perhaps submitting them on your business paper under the heading PRESS RELEASE will encourage the respective editors to include them in the news sections. This could be a useful and cost-effective way of promoting your consultancy.

Mailshots can be a very effective tool for marketing your consultancy. Study the detailed information about Mailshots on pages 44–45, and work out how you can incorporate this method into your marketing plans.

For more general marketing activity, do not be too rigid when targeting your material, particularly where you are offering services relating to universal subjects or interchangeable skills which could potentially cover several categories of business.

A useful tip: if your marketing activity is even more successful than you anticipated, have a contingency plan for excess work – you do not wish to be in the embarrassing situation of having to turn work away. Through your contacts with like-minded people, compile a list of those your consultancy could subcontract to; this way you can be prepared for overlapping jobs. Your contacts would no doubt be happy to reciprocate!

Image

Whichever marketing methods are used, a certain image of the business will be conveyed. An overriding aim should be to make sure that anybody's first contact with the business receives the right impression. This means that attention to detail is important. For example:

Premises

Whether you work from home or 'proper' business premises, an important and lasting impression of your business will be gained by people entering your office space for the first time.

Vehicles

Whether you use your own vehicle, which has a certain anonymity when driving along the road, or a commercial vehicle which has your company name painted on the side, an image is being conveyed to those who see it. If you arrive at a potential client's premises in a smart, clean vehicle, you are bound to create a more favourable image than if you arrive in a rusty old banger.

There is probably not a lot to worry about in the thought which could be in a prospective customer's mind, that if the business can afford to run such an exotic vehicle its fees or prices must be high. It is more likely to evoke the subconscious feeling that this must be a successful enterprise.

Telephone

Does your business have a policy about answering the telephone? If you *are* the business, who answers the telephone in your absence? Perhaps you have an answering machine: have you rung it up to see what your message sounds like – is it caller-friendly? Does it go on for too long? It can be very aggravating to a caller from a coinbox (not everyone has phonecards), particularly long distance, when the first coin runs out before the answering machine message is even finished.

A simple policy for your business to adopt could be to ensure that the caller realises quickly that the correct connection has been made, and that somebody is there willing and able to help – this is an excellent image-maker.

Letters

Consider the design of your stationery, not only what information needs to be on it, but how it is laid out. Have a look around at the display boards in the instant-print shops and you will see plenty of examples of what other businesses do. Some you will like, some you will not.

Try to decide what it is about those you like, and see how you could design yours to give an equally favourable impression on those who will be receiving it. While you are about it, think about having the letterheads, compliment slips and business cards all done together so that you have a continuity of design and presentation – again this is good for the image (see Chapter 9).

Having got a decent letterhead, do not spoil the effect by using it for unsightly letters. The layout of typewritten or word processed material, whether straightforward letters, price lists or other tabulated material, can say a lot about your business. Set a standard for the presentation of your written business matter, it can have no small influence on the image of your business (see Chapter 10).

Advertising matter

Whatever type of advertising matter you decide to adopt, do consider the general image it conveys of your business. Much of what has been said about the presentation of written material above, can be applied equally well to advertising matter. We will look at this subject in more detail shortly, but for the moment bear in mind that it has a role in presenting the image of a business as much as the actual product or service.

Personnel

Probably, when it really comes down to it, it is the people within the business who have the greatest effect on its image. A decently-designed piece of headed notepaper will look its best whatever is going on around it. People, however, are different, and respond, quite naturally, to their surroundings. This is why the people involved in the business must realise that their attitude and general demeanour will make or break the image of the business – even if this means on occasion submerging personal feelings.

We said at the beginning of this chapter that you need to let people know that your business exists. We have seen that this is not only done by the individuals within the business, that other, inanimate things have a bearing – but it must be true to say that in the end it is the actual people who create the most lasting image: every effort must be made to ensure that it is a favourable one.

CHAPTER **5** CHECKLIST

1 Your Marketing Profile
   - Have you completed your self-question checklist?

2 Marketing Methods
  Which is the best for your business?
   - Advertisements
   - Mailshots
   - Leaflet Drops
   - Personal Contact

3 Image
  What image do the following convey?
   - Your premises
   - Your vehicles
   - Your telephone answering person or machine
   - Your letters
   - Your advertising material
   - Your people

6

Selling the Product or Service

In this Chapter

Preparation

The approach

Establishing the customer's
    needs

Features and benefits

Objections

Closing

Additional sales and services

This chapter is not about retailing, where people come to you to buy. It is about selling your product or service to potential customers on their territory, or possibly on neutral territory, such as a hotel coffee lounge.

Preparation

Each potential customer is different, and will want to buy your product or service for slightly different reasons.

Find out as much as you can about the company or client – name, history, background, image, sales potential. Study their advertisements, their stationery and anything else which will give you information about them. You will have to fit into their image of themselves. For example, if when speaking to you or writing to you they have automatically called you by your first name, you know they will want the same approach from you. If their stationery is of top quality, and correspondence is well written and presented, it will tell you a lot about the client's or company's image of themselves. It will tell you, for example, that they or their employers invest time and money in creating a high-quality product or service. They will expect you to do the same.

Remember to take with you samples, leaflets, models – anything to enhance your own presentation. Take your business card and your diary, for future appointments.

Remind yourself of how this *particular* meeting was generated, especially if you have several calls to make, and have the names of the people you are going to meet firmly in your mind.

Set yourself an objective for this particular meeting, which might be one of several. For example, if this is your first meeting, your objective might be to set a date when you can demonstrate your product or meet the real decision maker. If it is a later meeting, your objective might be to clinch the sale. Do not expect to achieve everything in one meeting, particularly if you are after a sizeable contract, but do try to achieve the objective you have set yourself.

The approach

For a first meeting, the way you approach your potential client or customer is very important.

Unless you are meeting on neutral ground, you will be entering your customer's territory. Take note of whoever greets you: build up a friendly relationship with receptionists, secretaries and any other 'support' people. If you are visiting people's houses, remember to greet other members of the household if you meet them. Remember in both cases to say thank you for any refreshments provided. These people are all part of your customer's background and team, and can often be a help to you in the future.

Take note, too, of the environment. Is the place smart, tidy, fashionable, upmarket, disorganised, scruffy or what? Make allowances for working conditions in, say, a factory or warehouse and match your approach to the environment in which you find yourself. A chaotic place of work might mean a chaotic way of doing business. This is not to say that you must lower your standards in any way, but you should try to attune yourself to your customer's ambience.

Once you have greeted your customer with a handshake and called him or her by the appropriate name, you will probably be expected to make the opening remarks. It is useful to be able to refer to a letter you have written, or a leaflet or sample you have sent; have a spare copy handy in case yours has got mislaid by your customer. Do not at this stage try to go through all the good things about your product or service; it is very tempting to reel these off, but you might not be meeting the needs of that particular customer. Before trying to sell your product or service, you must establish what those needs are.

Establishing the customer's needs

You want to find out why your customer or client needs your product or service. To do this you must get your customer talking and be very clear in your mind how your product or service is going to meet those needs.

You could ask your customers to fill you in on what the requirements actually are. For example, if you are trying to land a contract to supply executive lunches in the boardroom, it would be helpful to know, *before* you start displaying your wares, whether this is a new idea for this company or whether they are dissatisfied with their present caterers, what sort of catering they had in mind and whether this is likely to be a one-off job or a longer contract. This information will then guide you into the sort of service you can offer and the cost before getting down to details of menu, time, numbers and so on.

To develop the conversation along informative lines, you will need to ask questions. Broadly speaking there are two sorts of questions – open and closed.

Open questions

These are questions which begin with words like *who*, *what*, *when*, *where*, *why* and *how*. They cannot be answered by a simple 'yes' or 'no', and force the person answering to give you at least some information. For example, 'How have you organised these lunches in the past?' might prompt the person to answer 'We haven't, this is a new idea', or 'Well, we've dropped them recently, because we weren't too happy with them'. You have gained a lot more information than if you had asked, 'Is this a new idea for you?' (a closed question), to which the reply could be either 'Yes' or 'No'.

Open questions are very useful for getting customers to open up and explain fully what their needs are.

Closed questions

As you have seen, these are questions which *can* invite a 'yes' or 'no' answer, and are less useful for drawing information out of people.

They can be useful if you want the customer to come to a decision, or make a choice. 'Would you prefer hot or cold?' will prompt either a definite choice or at least lead your customer down one road or the other. 'Shall I be here at 11.00 or 11.30?' stands more chance of getting a definite answer than 'What time would you like me here?'.

Continue questioning and clarifying until you are clear about what your customer or client actually wants. If it is obvious to you that what you have to offer does not in any way meet the requirements, it is better to say so than waste your time or your customer's by trying to sell something totally unsuitable or something that you cannot deliver. Do not be put off by objections (which are dealt with later in this chapter), nor by the customer's inability to see that your product or service would be of some benefit. Stop selling at this point only if you are quite sure your product or service is unacceptable.

Features and benefits

People buy for different reasons. At this point you have discovered what your client's or customer's real needs are. Now is the time to do two things: *describe the features* of your product or service, and *sell the benefits*.

The features are facts, the benefits are the good reasons why your customer should want your product or service – it is the benefits which you must sell.

To return to the executive luncheon service, listed below are some probable features and facts about the service and the allied benefits.

Executive Luncheon Service

Features	Benefits
All food prepared elsewhere and brought in	Client would save staff time buying in and preparing food

Waiter/waitress service	Prestige of expert attention to client's own customers
Wide choice of menu	Variety of tastes and dietary requirements catered for
All products bought fresh (not frozen, etc.)	Excellent quality of food
Large selection of wines	Flexible to meet cost requirements
All table preparation and cleaning done	No staff time taken

If your questioning revealed that these lunches had previously been done in-house, then you would emphasise the benefit of saving staff time. If it were a new idea for the company, you would mention the prestige attached to outside caterers.

You would not approach a potential customer or client without a full knowledge of your product or service, and what you can deliver; the skill is to match your product to the client's requirements by selling the benefits.

It is helpful to make a list of the features and likely benefits of your product or service so that you can call them quickly to mind in a selling situation.

Objections

A customer or client often has genuine objections to your product or service. Do not look upon this as an insurmountable obstacle, but as an opportunity to guide the client in the right direction by overcoming those objections.

Misunderstandings

Objections sometimes arise through misunderstandings or mis-interpretations in both directions. If a customer says something like 'Yes, but I'm not too sure . . .' try to find out where the uncertainty lies by asking questions and probing into the area of doubt. It might be that the customer has misheard or mis-read something, or that you have not explained it clearly. It might be that you have not understood what the client meant. Keep clarifying until you do, and then clear up the misunderstanding.

For example, if the 'Executive Luncheon' client said, 'I'm not too sure about salmon mousse as a starter', it might be that you had given the impression that salmon mousse was the only starter available or that you had not understood that the client does not like fish. In either event by asking, 'What would you prefer as a starter?' you will probably elicit enough information to clear up the point.

> Misunderstandings?   clarify and explain

Scepticism

Sometimes customers or clients are doubtful about the capacity of your product or service to meet their needs. If they say something like 'Yes, but I can't see how . . .' you must reassure them by proving that your product or service will meet their needs.

This is the time to quote definite facts or demonstrate the product. You can show relevant tables of figures, make good estimates of time and/or money saved or literally demonstrate the product there and then.

If the 'Executive Luncheon' client said, 'I don't see how you can get the boardroom clear in a quarter of an hour', you could quote other examples (named clients) of where you had done just that, or you could take the client quickly through the timings, emphasising the fact that everything is brought in easily-packed trays.

> Scepticism?   give proof

Price

One of the most common objections is the cost. You must be very sure in your own mind how low you can go in accepting a lower cost, and be flexible down to that point. You can emphasise the fact that VAT is recoverable (if it is); you should also re-state the agreed benefits to the customer.

You might be able to go lower on one point (perhaps reduce the delivery charge) while sticking on another. Sometimes it is better to quote for the whole package, while emphasising what the package contains. At others it is useful to 'unbundle' the package (cost each element separately) so the client can buy at least some of it.

Try not to let the customer buy only the least profitable parts of the package. For example, the 'Executive Luncheon' firm would be unwise to let the client provide the wine, because that is probably the most profitable part of the business. However, if such a deal were to lead to a long and good contract, the firm might decide to let it go this time and re-negotiate another time.

Price?   remind the customer of the agreed benefits
be prepared to negotiate, but know your limits

Closing

The customer will eventually give an indication that (s)he is ready to bring the meeting to a close. The signs might be verbal: 'Well, if you would like to let me have a copy of those figures for Monday morning . . .' or 'Yes, I like what you're offering, but I need to consult my colleagues'. The signs might be non-verbal – nodding; leaning forward, hands on thighs; standing up. A good book on body language and how it can help a salesperson is *Body Language* by Allan Pease, published by Sheldon Press and obtainable from most good bookshops.

When you receive these closing signals, STOP SELLING. More than one sale has been lost by the salesperson over-emphasising agreed benefits or, worse still, introducing benefits not mentioned before, which only confuse the customer. It is not easy to stop yourself from telling the customer *all* the benefits of your product or service, but once the closing signals have been given, you must stop selling.

Summarise what has been agreed between you. If a new meeting is to be arranged, try to arrange it then and there – get your diary out and suggest dates and times. If a senior executive asks you to make an appointment with his or her secretary, make it with the secretary and do not try to force the executive to make the appointment. If you are to provide further information, establish exactly when and where it is to be delivered. If your customer is to let you have further information, try to get a definite commitment on what it is and the anticipated timing. If the person to whom you are speaking is not the decision-maker, try to make sure that your product or service gets presented to the decision maker. Try to get a name, and offer to write or meet to demonstrate the product – anything to take the matter a step further.

If you are able to clinch the sale at that meeting, make sure that *all* costs, delivery dates and so on are agreed, and get a signature if possible. Immediately after the meeting write and confirm the terms of the agreement, set out very clearly what you are supplying, what the costs are and what the terms of payment are (see Chapter 7). If you think it more than likely that this meeting will be the one where you finally make the sale, you can have all this paperwork ready with you, but do not produce it too early in the proceedings.

At the close of the meeting, each party should be clear about what is to happen next on both sides. This applies to a service rendered in someone's home just as much as it does to a product sold to a large company. Shake hands to conclude the meeting.

As you leave, remember to say goodbye to support staff or other members of the household, and thank them for anything they have done for you.

Finally, when you get back to your own place of work, do everything that you have promised to do, and do it promptly.

Additional sales and services

Sometimes there is an opportunity to offer additional sales or services; the skill here lies in seizing the opportunity but not being too pushy about it.

You might be able, in the course of selling a package, to suggest a small extra which would enhance the end product or service and make extra sales for you. The 'Executive Luncheon' firm might be able to introduce their printed menu service; a secretarial bureau might suggest thermal binding to enhance the presentation of a proposal.

If you cannot introduce these additional sales and services during the selling process, you might be able to leave a leaflet or some other advertising material as you conclude your business. Never travel without your publicity material, and leave it behind if possible, without forcing it on your customers or clients.

CHAPTER 6 CHECKLIST

1 Preparation
- What do you know about your potential client or customer?
- Who are you going to meet?
- Have you got everything you need,
  including publicity material for additional sales and services?
- What are your objectives for this meeting?

2 Approach
- Build relationships with 'support' people
- Note the environment
- Shake hands and use the appropriate name
- Refer to something already done or sent

3 Establish needs
- Ask questions: *open* questions help to clarify
  closed questions help choices and decisions
- Get the customer talking

4 Features and benefits
- Make a list of the features and benefits of your product or service
- Describe the features/facts – demonstrate if appropriate
- Sell the benefits

5 Objections
- Misunderstanding – clarify and explain
- Scepticism – give proof
- Price – remind the customer of the agreed benefits
  be prepared to negotiate, but know your limits

6 Closing
- Stop selling
- Summarise what has been agreed
- Agree action plan

---

7 Additional sales and service
- Introduce during the selling process if possible
- Leave publicity material at the conclusion of the meeting, but do not force it

8 DID YOU ACHIEVE YOUR OBJECTIVE?

7

Doing the Books

In this Chapter

Receipts and payments

Petty Cash

VAT

Banking

Necessary/useful records

Manual or computer

Year end

Next to stocktaking, many business people consider doing the books a necessary chore. The key to successful, and not excessively time-consuming, book-keeping is to have a workable system, to keep to it, and so keep on top of the workload.

Receipts and payments

Broadly speaking, the books of a business are divided into two sections, one to record moneys coming in and the other to record moneys going out. An average small business does not need to have a complicated system of book-keeping, but it does need to show clearly the incomings and outgoings of the business, and dates when the transactions took place.

A very simple system could look like this (see opposite):

However, in use it would not be very practical, because it is useful to analyse receipts and payments (particularly payments) under different headings at the time of recording the details in the books: this can be done with very little effort or trouble.

A basic loose-leaf accounts system has advantages for a new

RECEIPTS				PAYMENTS			
Date	Description	£	p	Date	Description	£	p

business. It is worth making a visit to a shop which specialises in this type of business stationery and studying the options. There are some well-known brand names in this area. Decide what you want your account sheets to do, and find the most appropriate ones for the job.

For the main record keeping, a standard 11¾ ins × 14 ins (297 × 356 mm) sheet with four columns for receipts and 16 columns for payments would probably be suitable.

A basic loose leaf account layout could look something like the example on page 64:

A typical payment entry made by cheque would show, apart from the date and who was being paid, the gross amount in the Total Bank column (Column 1), the amount of VAT (Column 3), with the net amount in the appropriate analysis column (Columns 4–16). If there was no VAT involved, the amount in the analysis column would be the same as that in the Total Bank Column.

It is sometimes possible that items in one transaction apply to more than one analysis column. In this case, enter the amounts in the appropriate columns, and check to see that everything adds across to the figure in the Total Bank column (Column 1).

A suitable breakdown of payments could be as follows, with each heading having its own column across the page:

Materials	Entertainment
Light/heat	Subsistence/hotel
Petrol/travel	Capital equipment
Vehicle expenses	Advertising
Telephone and postage	Rent/rates
Printing and stationery	Insurances

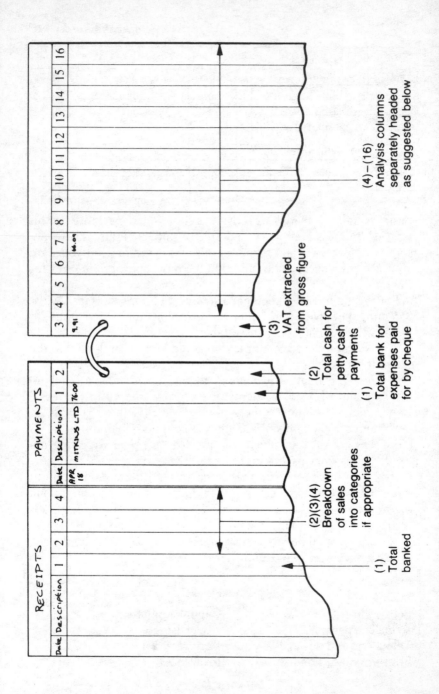

It would also be useful to segregate out payments like:

Bank charges and interest
Money withdrawn from the bank for Petty Cash replenishment
DSS deductions
Inland Revenue payments
Payments of VAT to HM Customs and Excise (see VAT heading page 68)

Another necessary column would show any Drawings or directors' fees made from the business account for personal use.

One indispensible column for those payments which for one reason or another will not fit into any other column is the one headed Sundries, and would probably be the final one on the sheet.

If you find you need more headings than will comfortably fit into columns 4 to 16 on one sheet, use a second analysis sheet. Ask your accountant to advise you on the headings most appropriate to your business.

Cross-check all figures each time a sheet is completed. It is worth taking time to do this so that any errors in calculation can be highlighted quickly, and you can move onto the new sheet confident that all is accurate.

As well as totalling each sheet as it is completed, the sheets should be ruled off at suitable intervals – weekly, monthly, quarterly – depending on what is most appropriate for your business.

As supplementary sheets for recording Sales or Petty Cash, a standard 11¾ ins × 8¼ ins (297 × 210 mm) sheet with four or five columns would enable you to record the facts needed.

For example, for Invoiced Sales:

	INVOICED SALES		(1)	(2)	(3)	(4)
Date	Description	INV.	Gross	VAT	Net	Payment received
MAR 21	DECEMM LTD	3821	702.53	91.63	610.90	MAY 8

66

Having a Payment Received column (Column 4) enables you to see at a glance how many outstanding invoices there are at any one time.

If your business is involved in Cash Sales, you would probably find it easier and more convenient to keep a separate record sheet for those.

A Petty Cash Record could be as straightforward as this:

PETTY CASH RECORD			(1)	(2)	(3)	(4)
Date	Description	Week no.	IN	OUT	Balance	
	Opening balance		25.00	—	25.00	
w/e MAR6	EXPENSES	①		6.10	18.90	
w/e MAR13	EXPENSES	②		12.19	6.71	
MAR21	REPLENISHMENT		50.00		56.71	

It is, as you can see, a control or summary sheet. It is a very useful way of keeping an eye on the balance, to know when the Petty Cash float needs replenishing.

We will look at the detail behind these expense figures under the Petty Cash section of this chapter, page 67.

If it suits the pattern of your business, for both these sheets you could rule them off each month. Apart from anything else, it means if the figures do not balance, there is only one month's work to check!

Petty Cash

Petty Cash is a sum of money used for small, everyday expense items. These day-to-day business expenses need to be properly recorded.

It is a good practical idea to have a small (160 × 100 mm) Cash Book, which it is easy to carry about, in which to record expenses as they happen. It is a very useful habit to get into. For example, when you buy the train ticket, or the supply of postage stamps, write the amount in your Petty Cash book straight away.

At the end of, say, each week, the details of the expenses in your Petty Cash book are recorded on the main account sheet, with the total figure of each expenditure being written in the Total Cash column (Column 2) with any VAT in column 3 and the net figures in the appropriate analysis column (Columns 4–16).

The total amount of the weekly expenditure is recorded on the Petty Cash Record sheet. This is best done when the money is actually paid out: it also provides a good opportunity to check the balance in the Petty Cash tin.

When the money has been reclaimed, the Petty Cash book should be marked accordingly. Simply writing 'Reimbursed' across the entries in red ink could be sufficient.

Try and maintain a system to ensure that each expense claim is accompanied by a receipt. This is not possible in all cases, of course; parking meters will not issue a receipt (even though Traffic Wardens could provide another type of document in certain circumstances!), but a Pay and Display and multi-storey car park will provide a receipt. You have to hand in your train ticket at the barrier, but the Post Office clerk will give you a receipt for your stamps if asked: complications can arise in a restaurant if a group of you wish to have separate bills for your own account records – try mentioning this fact when ordering your meals.

If something is bought in a retail shop as a Petty Cash expense, it is important that the receipt shows the VAT number of that business. Many, though not all, till receipts show the VAT number of the business issuing it. It is always worth checking, and if there is no number, ask for a VAT receipt.

VAT (value added tax)

VAT is the tax on goods and services as supplied. It is administered on behalf of the government by HM Customs and Excise (see Chapter 9). We are concerned here about recording VAT in the books of the business. Even if you are not yet registered for VAT yourself, it could still be worthwhile isolating the VAT from your payments, because it may be possible to claim some of it in retrospect when you do register; ask your accountant's advice on this. In any case it is all good practice, and a useful habit to get into.

You, as a business, can only be charged VAT by another organisation if that business is itself VAT registered. A VAT registered company must show its nine digit VAT registration number (set out like this: 987 6543 21) on its stationery, particularly its invoices and receipts.

The point is that a VAT registered company can claim back the VAT it has paid on legitimate business expenses. We will cover the method of doing this later in this section.

As far as the books are concerned, the principle of recording an expense involving VAT so as to isolate the VAT figure would be like this

Date	Description	Gross	VAT	Net
Aug 23	ENVELOPES	1.25	0.16	1.09

Note: This is assuming a VAT rate of 15%.
For a list of what is acceptable as a business expense, see Chapter 8.

On an accounts sheet with analysis columns, the £1.09 would be written in the Stationery column.

When making these entries it is useful to check the maths by cross-casting the figures across the line to ensure that the net figure plus the VAT equals the gross amount. This can save a lot of time – and heartache – when you get to the bottom of the account sheet and have to reconcile all the figures.

It is probably worthwhile at this stage to look at the mechanics of extracting the VAT from a VAT-inclusive price, where the VAT amount is not shown as a separate figure (although an increasing number of till receipts do this).

We will use our envelopes as an example. Basing the calculation on 15% VAT, the figures are:

VAT-inclusive price	1.25
15% VAT	0.16
VAT-exclusive price	£1.09

The answer is easy to see, but how is it arrived at? The solution is not as easy as taking 15% away from the VAT-inclusive price, because 15% of £1.25 is more than 15% of £1.09 (which is the figure we want).

If you do this on a calculator: $1.25 \times 15\% -$ (minus sign) you will see that the answer is 0.1875 and not 0.1630 as it should be.

What you have to do is a calculation which is directly related to the VAT rate, and which will change whenever the VAT rate changes. For a 15% rate the calculation is:

$$\text{VAT-inclusive price} \times 3 \div 23$$

Apply this to our example:

$$1.25 \times 3 = 3.75 \div 23 = 0.1630$$

Therefore 1.25 minus 0.16 equals 1.09.

The fraction for 15% VAT is $\frac{3}{23}$, but remember to find out what the new fraction is if the VAT rate changes.

It is important to be able to do this calculation because, although some amounts may be small, if they are added together with the claims for other purchases or expenses (for instance, petrol and parking) they can soon add up to a significant amount.

VAT Returns are made quarterly to HM Customs and Excise. On your VAT Return form you fill in the value of the supplies you have made and received during the tax period, and pay the total tax you owe to HM Customs and Excise, or claim a repayment if tax is owed to you (which can happen if your expenses have been greater than your receipts).

The VAT Return, and any payment due must reach HM Customs and Excise by the due date shown on the Return: penalties could be incurred for late payment, particularly if this is consistently happening.

The following extracts from notes supplied by HM Customs and Excise may provide you with some helpful general background information about VAT.

It is the *person*, not the business, who is registered for VAT. Each registration covers *all* the business activities of the registered person.

The *person* to be registered can be a sole proprietor, a partnership (including husband and wife partnerships), a limited company, a club or association, or a charity.

If you are a taxable person, you must account for VAT whenever you make a taxable supply. The supply is your *output* and the VAT is your *output tax*.

If your customer is registered for VAT and the supply is for the purpose of business, the supply is his *input* and the tax you charge him is his *input tax*. In the same way, VAT charged to you on your business purchases is your input tax.

There are many helpful leaflets describing the various aspects of VAT published by HM Customs and Excise. It is worthwhile paying a visit to your local VAT office – addresses are in The phone Book under 'Customs and Excise'.

All your dealings should be with your local VAT office; you only deal with the Head Office at Southend when you send them back your Quarterly Return.

Banking

A new business needs to have its own bank account, and arrangements should be made to open at least a current account. There are a few basic things to be considered and arranged:

You will not receive a cheque guarantee card with a business account – although you can have a cashpoint card.

You will need to provide a sum of money to deposit into the account to make it active (this would be recorded on the account sheets as 'capital introduced').

If there is to be more than one signatory, arrangements should be made with the bank about whether all should sign or whether any one of those designated is sufficient. In any case sample signatures from all signatories will need to be provided.

You will receive a bank statement each month. You may have to ask for this because banks will sometimes only send statements quarterly, particularly for private accounts. This is too long a period for a business account.

Consider whether you need to have an overdraft facility attached to this account. Find out what the arrangement fee will be, and how long the arrangement is to last before it is reviewed; negotiate for as long a period as possible.

The name of the bank account needs to be decided. Will it be in the name of the business only, or perhaps in the name of the sole trader? Will it have the name of the person and the business name, for instance Arthur Cosford T/A ARCO SERVICES?

A paying in book will be necessary for depositing cheques and moneys received by the business.

A business bank account is bound to attract bank charges, even if it is only after an interest-free period, which some banks advertise for new business accounts. You will recall we suggested having a column to record these on the account analysis sheets. You may be paying interest charges from the start.

Consider whether you need to open a deposit account, where moneys not immediately needed could be placed to earn some interest. This, or any other suitable form of interest-earning account could be useful for putting aside moneys in anticipation of the next VAT Return. Remember, if you charge VAT on your goods or supplies, a proportion of the money you receive (15% at present) will be required by HM Customs and Excise. Beware of thinking you are better off than you really are and unwittingly spending your VAT money.

Bank statements
When you receive a bank statement for your business account, you need to check the details against the entries on your account sheets. This need not be a complicated exercise; simply tick (in red so that it will show up easily) the statement and the equivalent entry on your account sheets. Keep each statement carefully with your records, your accountant will need them when auditing your books.

You may well find items on the bank statement which you have not recorded on your account sheets. The bank charges and/or interest will probably be one. In this case, write in the amount on the account sheet and tick both this entry and the statement. It can be useful to include in the entry on the account sheets the statement number where the charges appeared; this could well help your accountant reconcile the figures at some future date.

This is quite a useful general principle to follow when doing the books: ask yourself when writing in a transaction, 'Will this make sense to somebody looking at it sometime in the future?' (your accountant, the VAT man, the Inland Revenue). If there is any doubt at all, make a little note as a reminder – it could save you a grilling from any of the above-mentioned parties, with you racking your brains trying to remember the details or circumstances.

Other items on a business bank statement which have not been recorded on your account sheets could be direct debit deduction – for instance DSS Insurance. These can vary in amount, depending on the number of weeks in the month covered by the statement. As before, write the details onto your account sheets – allocate a separate column to record these outgoings – tick them, and note the statement number on the account sheet for future reference.

Security
Your business activities will no doubt involve you in making visits to the bank from time to time. If you need to make regular visits, particularly for the purpose of depositing or withdrawing cash, consider the security implications, not only for the money but for yourself or your personnel.

Simple devices like varying the time and the route, and perhaps the people, could help to avoid any unpleasantness en route.

Necessary or useful records

Records and various statistics are kept and maintained by a business. These will obviously vary according to the type of business, and the use which can be made of the data they contain.

We have tried to prepare a checklist of those records it is necessary – even legal – to keep, and those which it could be useful to have. Use it as a basis for compiling one which would be relevant for your business.

Necessary	Useful
Accounting sheets and ancillary documents	Breakdown of sales – by time or product or both
Bank statements	Comparison figures – between
Receipts for payments made	different parts of the business
Sales invoices	or last week/last year
VAT records, including VAT Returns	

Manual or computer

What we have described in this chapter is a basic manual system for doing the books, which will probably be the best way to start.

As your business progresses and expands, you may well consider developing its systems to something more mechanical – take your accountant's advice before you embark on anything definite.

The sort of thing which might be suitable to consider is an accounts package on a personal computer. Systems vary in sophistication. You can get systems and details in which for your *sales*, you key in the amount of goods supplied and details about price, settlement terms, VAT rates and so on and the system will do all the calculations for you, print out an Invoice and add the required amount to your VAT Return at the end of the quarter.

For *purchases*, again you key in the details of the purchase and how payment is to be made; the system will produce a list of cheques to be made out (sometimes the cheques themselves). The amount of VAT you can claim will be automatically added to your VAT Return. The total of your net sales and purchases are then added as the actual figures on your Cash Flow Forecast (see Chapter 2) so that you can see at a glance how well your business is doing.

Do not rush into buying computer software for your book-keeping, particularly if you are fairly new to computers. You need to buy the software which is right for your business, or you might decide in the end to computerise only part of it.

Make sure that you keep computerised records carefully. Make back-up disks in case your current disks get corrupted. Your accountant will need your summary printouts (which can usually be automatically generated by the system) for the audit trail. HM

Customs and Excise and the Inland Revenue might require these as well.

If you are running a business with many customer accounts requiring lots of Invoices each month, a computerised book-keeping system could save you a lot of time. If you are running, say, a consultancy with far fewer invoices and payments, the amount of time saved is minimal.

The other type of package which you might find very useful is a wages package. Once set up, this can, with a minimal amount of keying in, generate pay slips and cheques, so that you know your employees receive all the information and money to which they are entitled (see Chapter 11).

Year end

At the end of your company's financial year, you will have to submit all your books and accounts to your accountant to audit and present to the Inland Revenue. You will not be able to do this until the final bank statement for the year has arrived and been included in your accounts for that year.

If yours is a limited company, remember that the accounts must be submitted to Companies House not later than nine months after the end of the financial year, so it helps your accountant if you are prompt in completing and delivering the year's books or computer printouts.

CHAPTER 7 CHECKLIST
1 You need to record all transactions. Have you got adequate records, on paper or computer, of the following:
   (a) Sales – goods and services you sell
   (b) Purchases – goods and services you buy
   (c) Banking transactions
   (d) Petty cash
   (e) VAT Returns?
2 How frequently do you do your books?
3 Does your system let you know how well your business is doing?

8

Personal Finances and Business Expenses

In this Chapter

Money for personal use   Income tax
NI contributions and   Allowable business expenses
  pensions

In Chapter 2, we considered the financial aspects of relating to your product or service. In this chapter we will be looking at various financial implications relating to the individual, especially the way they affect the person who is self employed. Many of these financial impositions have a legal liability.

NB The information in this chapter was correct in 1989. Check with your accountant about subsequent changes.

Money for personal use

In Chapter 7, we saw that a column is reserved for Drawings or directors' salary: moneys which are withdrawn from the business for personal use. As a sole trader or a member of a partnership, this could well be done on an as-and-when basis. With a limited company, it is more likely to take the form of a regular amount drawn from the company account in the form of a salary.

Credit cards: credit cards with no credit limit (for instance *Amex* and *Diners*) can be very useful, particularly if you have to travel a lot. If you think you need one of these and are employed, but about to be self-employed, get your card *before* you leave your full-time employment. It is much easier to get one of these cards if you are employed.

NI contributions and pensions

Almost everybody who is self employed pays towards a basic state pension through making National Insurance (NI) contributions. In Chapter 7, we showed how you should record these on your account sheets if you are paying by Direct Debit. There are numerous methods of payment – ask the DSS for details.

The amount you pay depends partly on the amount of your taxable business profits from £2300 per year (1989 figures). Some is paid by monthly contributions and some is paid at the same time as your Income Tax. Ask your accountant for details.

Self-employed people cannot get SERPS (State Earnings Related Pension Scheme), on the basic state pension. If you are self employed you can get tax relief on payments to a Personal Pension Plan (PPP). This is one of the best forms of investment you can make. Do your pension sums well ahead of retirement: once your pension starts to be paid, you will not be able to take a cash lump sum.

Income tax

To be treated as self employed for tax purposes, you must convince your tax office (preferably through your accountant) that you are genuinely in business on your own account, and not an employee. This will depend, amongst other things, on whether you risk your own money or provide major items of equipment, whether you are told what to do, where, when and how – or decide by yourself.

Each Inland Revenue and DSS local office has someone responsible for saying whether or not you will be treated as self employed. Inland Revenue leaflet IR56 has more details.

If you form a limited company, the tax rules are quite different; you pay corporation tax on the business profits, and you will need the help of your accountant to deal with this.

Sole traders and partnerships are taxed in a similar way, but there are special rules for partnerships.

In a partnership the partners are each responsible for the tax on their own income not related to the partnership. The partnership also gets its own tax return. The profit is then divided between the individual partners in proportion to what each gets under the partnership agreement. Each partner's share is taxed at his or her own rate of tax, taking into account other personal income and allowances. If one partner does not pay his or her share, the others are liable to pay it on his or her behalf.

If there is a change in the members of the partnership, tax may be charged on the *actual profits* in the year of the change and the following three years, instead of on a preceding year basis.

Allowable business expenses

You can deduct *allowable* business expenses from your profits. An expense will be allowable only if it is incurred 'wholly and exclusively' for the business. This does not mean that you can claim nothing if, for example, you use your car partly for business and partly for private purposes, or use part of your home for business.

You can normally claim the proportion of these costs that is attributable to business use – you will have to agree the proportion with your tax office (preferably via your accountant).

Car expenses are usually shared out according to mileage.

If you are self employed (or have some freelance or sparetime work) and do part of your work at home, you can normally claim, as an allowable expense, the proportion of the cost of running your home attributable to business use. You will have to agree with your tax office – through your accountant – what proportion of telephone, heating bills etc. you can claim.

If you devote part of your home, a room, say, exclusively to business use, you should be able to claim a proportion of rent and rates – usually based on the number and size of rooms, BUT exclusive use for business purposes may mean some capital gains tax to pay when you sell – check with your accountant.

Circumstances vary considerably, but the sort of business expenses which might be allowable – or not allowable – could be:

78

Normally allowed	Not allowed
Basic costs and general running expenses:	Initial cost of:
	• machinery
Cost of goods bought for re-sale and raw materials used in business	• vehicles
Advertising	• equipment
Delivery charges	• permanent advertising signs
Heating and lighting	
Cleaning	
Rates and rent of business premises	
Telephone and postage	
Replacement of small tools and special clothing	
Stationery	
Relevant books and magazines	
Accountant's fees	
Bank charges on business accounts	
Subscriptions to professional and trade organisations	
Use of home for work:	
Proportion of:	
• telephone	
• lighting	
• heating	
• cleaning	
• insurance	
Proportion of rent and rates if part of home is used *exclusively* for business (but beware of Capital Gains Tax)	
Wages and salaries:	
Wages, salaries, redundancy and reasonable leaving payments paid to employees	Your own wages or salary or that of any partner
Pensions for ex-employees and their dependents	
Training costs for employees to	

Normally allowed	Not allowed
acquire or improve skills needed for their current job, and re-training costs for employees who are leaving	
Tax and National Insurance:	
Employers National Insurance contributions for employees	Income tax
	Capital Gains tax
VAT on allowable business expenses if you are a VAT registered trader	Inheritance tax
	Your own National Insurance contributions
Entertaining:	
Entertainment of your own staff	Any business entertaining
Gifts:	
Gifts costing up to £10 a year per person, so long as the gift advertises your business	Food, drink, tobacco gifts or vouchers for goods given to anyone other than employees
Gifts of any value to employees	
Insurance:	
Business insurance premiums e.g.	Premiums for your own:
• Employer's liability	• Life insurance
• Fire and theft	• Accident insurance
• Motor	• Sickness insurance
• Employees' Life Cover	
Travelling and subsistence:	
Cost of travel and accommodation on business trips	Travel between home and business
Reasonable cost of dinner and breakfast – but not lunch – on overnight trips	Cost of buying car or van
Travel between different places of work	
Running costs of own car: whole of cost, excluding depreciation if used privately too	

80

Normally allowed	Not allowed
Interest payments:	
Interest on, and costs of arranging, overdrafts and loans for business purposes	Interest on capital paid or credited to partners Interest on overdue tax
Hiring:	
Reasonable charge for hire of capital goods, including cars	
Trade marks, designs and patents:	
Fees paid to register trade mark or design, or to obtain a patent	Cost of buying patent
Legal costs:	
Cost of • recovering debts • defending business rights • preparing service agreements • appealing against rates on business premises • renewing lease, with landlord's consent, for 50 years or less (but not if premium paid)	Expenses (including stamp duty) for acquiring land, buildings or leases Fines and other penalties for breaking the law Costs of fighting a tax case
Repairs:	
Normal repairs and maintenance to premises or equipment	Costs of additions, alterations or improvements
Subscriptions/contributions:	
Payments which secure benefits for your business and staff Genuine contribution to approved local Enterprise Agency Payments to professional bodies which have arrangements with the Inland Revenue (in some cases only a proportion of the payment can be claimed)	Payments to: • political parties • churches • charities (Small gifts to *local* charities may be allowable)

Normally allowed	Not allowed
Capital expenditure:	
	Capital expenditure (i.e. what you spend on buying cars, machinery, etc.) is not an allowable expense
	Depreciation of equipment (This would be dealt with by your accountant under Capital Allowances)

CHAPTER **8** CHECKLIST

1 What arrangements have you made for drawing money out of your company for personal expenditure?

2 What arrangements have you made to pay your NI contributions?

3 Which personal pension plan do you have? If none, start to make arrangements now.

4 Have you agreed with the Inland Revenue and the DSS that you are self-employed?

5 Do you claim *all* allowable business expenses?

6 Do you claim any business expenses which are not allowable? If you do, the Inland Revenue can say that your books are incorrect, and can ask to see and check everything in great detail.

9

The Professionals

In this Chapter

How to find the
  professionals

Accountants

Architects

Banks and building societies

Estate agents

HM Customs and Excise
  (VAT)

Insurance brokers

Printers

Secretarial services

Solicitors

This chapter outlines the specialist services you may need to help you set up your business, to expand it and to keep it going. Some of the things listed here you may be able to do for yourself, but when you need professional help, get the best you can afford.

How to find the professionals

You should be able to find all these professional services listed in Yellow Pages, Thomson's and other local directories, but how do you know which one to pick?

You often know or have used the services of at least one of these before – a banker or a solicitor perhaps. If they seem to be business-like and helpful, they are a good place to start, and can often recommend other services. For example, a banker can sometimes recommend an accountant, an estate agent can recommend an architect or a printer can recommend some secretarial services.

Your Local Enterprise Agency can perhaps point you in the right direction, and your public library often has lists available. Read the advertisements in the local and national newspaper to see what banks and building societies are offering, or look under the Classified Advertisements for services such as printers and accountants. You will find the local VAT office in the telephone directory under HM Customs and Excise.

Probably the best source of finding the right professional advice is the personal recommendation of someone you know and trust. Very large organisations, such as banks and building societies, do tend to vary, depending on the local manager.

Accountants

A good accountant will be one of your best assets. Accountants can render the following main services:

- Book-keeping (see Chapter 7)
- VAT returns
- Annual trading accounts
- Tax returns
- Help with Cash Flow forecasts

Many small businesses do the book-keeping and VAT returns themselves and leave their accountant to do the more complicated jobs of the annual trading accounts and negotiations with the Inland Revenue. A qualified accountant is essential for Limited Companies.

Do not expect an accountant to present your annual accounts to you within about a month of the end of your financial year. They usually take a great deal longer than this (up to a year), but you should expect them to deal promptly with Inland Revenue matters; if they do not, you might have to pay interest on unpaid tax.

Architects

You may never need the services of a qualified architect, but you might need:

- a professional survey of property you want to rent or buy
- plans properly drawn up for local planning permission purposes.

These might be necessary just for a sign on someone else's building or jutting out over the pavement

Banks and building societies

These are under one heading because they seem to provide similar services. However, for businesses they can be very different.

You cannot at this time open a small business account with a Building Society – their accounts are strictly for personal use. This means that if you open a Building Society account as a sole trader or a small partnership, you will not have your business name on your cheques, and you are unlikely to be able to get overdrafts as and when you need them. You can open an account in your own name, or perhaps with one or two partners in private names, and use the account as though you were a private individual or individuals. If you do this, be sure to request that transactions are valid on one signature only. You would have to keep strict records that the money belongs to the company, and seek the advice of your accountant on tax returns.

All the major banks are very eager to help small businesses. They all have start-up packs, with help and advice on book-keeping procedures, banking procedures and so on. You are unlikely to have to pay bank charges during your first trading year.

Through your bank account you can deal with:

- Standing Orders
- Direct Debits (including the monthly payment to the DSS for your National Insurance)
- Credit transfers
- Cheque payments with a company cheque (no cheque guarantee card)
- Cash withdrawal (for Petty Cash purposes) by cash card

Make sure you get your bank statements at frequent intervals (monthly, not quarterly) so that you can keep your book-keeping up-to-date.

Your bank manager will also be a good source of funding for the business if the case is properly presented (see Chapter 2) and will grant reasonable overdrafts to ease cashflow problems.

You can open a Deposit Account in your business name, and

make arrangements for sums to be transferred to and from it as required. Your bank manager likes to see your money earning money.

On the payment side, after a year you will probably have to pay bank charges. Ask the bank for a breakdown of how these are calculated. If you arrange an overdraft, you will have to pay an arrangement fee – so the longer the arrangement, the better. Be sure to ask what the interest rates will be, and try to negotiate a lower rate if possible; these are not fixed charges.

If you are paid by cheque which bounces ('Return to Drawer'), the onus is on you to:

- instruct your bank not to re-present the cheque to your customer's bank
- chase the customer yourself

If you do not do this, your bank will go on re-presenting the cheque and charging you every time it does so.

Do not be misled into thinking that because you pay a cheque into your bank account at your own branch it will always be cleared on that day. It will often take two working days to clear. If, for example, you transfer money from your Building Society into your bank account and on the same day write a cheque which is presented on that day or the next, it could be that the cheque is processed *before* your transfer is credited to your account, and you will be charged interest on 'insufficient funds'. This can happen quite easily over a weekend.

Like a good accountant, a helpful bank manager can be a great asset, in spite of the charges which sometimes seem hidden to the unwary. Do ask you bank manager for help and advice: many banks have people specially assigned to small business enterprises.

Estate agents

As already mentioned (see Chapter 3) there are usually estate agents who specialise in business premises. They will be able to advise you on:

- What is available
- Local developments

- Local planning restrictions
- The size of premises which are right for your business
- The best locality for your business

They will also be able to draw up inventories for you, if necessary, on fixtures and fittings which are part of the purchase or lease of the property.

Generally speaking estate agents do not, at the present time, deal with conveyancing, leasing or rental agreements.

HM Customs and Excise (VAT)

It might seem strange to list the VAT man under 'Professionals', but in fact your VAT man can be very helpful to you. As it says in Chapter 7, you may choose to become VAT registered, even if your turnover is under the limit of £23,500 per annum (1989 figures). Once you have decided to register, you cannot choose to become de-registered.

Your local VAT office can give very good advice on what is and is not liable to VAT, for both charging and claiming purposes, and what is zero-rated. They will also advise you on how you should show calculations on invoices, particularly where there is a mixture of VAT rates and complications such as discounts and carriage charges.

The VAT man has the right to enter your business premises (even when you work from home) at any time to check your books. Usually they make an appointment, and give you time to arrange to have your accountant with you if you wish. Like the Inland Revenue, if they find one mistake in your books, they are able to say that the Returns are incorrect, and go through everything with a fine-tooth comb. The VAT men do not set out to be oppressive, but they are strict and efficient; they are always willing to help, if asked.

Insurance brokers

Insurance brokers are the middlemen between you and insurance companies; they do all the work of finding the right insurance policies for your needs.

Under the Financial Services Act, they are by law required to give you 'best advice'. Although they earn their money by being paid commission by the insurance companies, they should not recommend a particular company if that is not the best one for you.

They should be able to advise you on the type of insurance you need for your business, for example:

Buildings	Goods in transit
Contents	Your own life
Special cover	Loss of earnings through
Vehicles	accident or illness
Public liability	Professional negligence
Employer's liability	(doctors, lawyers, architects,
(if you employ others)	counsellors, etc.)

There are often brokers or insurance companies which specialise in your type of business; you can probably get their names through personal recommendation from other people in the same line of business as yourself.

Printers

If you are not used to designing logos, letterheads, packaging and other similar materials, you can seek the advice of a professional marketing consultant (see Chapter 5). If you are starting off in a very small way, ask your printer for advice.

Printers like to see their products looking good, and they have an eye for these things. They can advise you on such things as:

- quality, size and colour of paper and envelopes
- layout of letterheads
- size of typeface

Some printers run a start-up pack for small businesses, and will provide you with a small amount of letterheads, envelopes, business cards and compliment slips to get you started (see Chapter 10).

A small printer is a good idea to begin with, because you will not want more than about a ream (480–500 sheets) of printed stationery in case you change your mind about your logo, name and address etc. Larger printers tend to work on large orders.

Printers often run a photocopying service and can recommend secretarial services.

Secretarial services

There is usually a word processing or secretarial services bureau somewhere in your area, or a professional typist working from home. You can find them in Yellow Pages or the Classified Advertisements section of your local paper.

They will produce top quality letters, envelopes, labels, reports, proposals, business plans. They should also check and amend your English, if necessary, and even re-write or compose letters etc. for you; checking spelling and grammar is generally part of the service, but re-phrasing or composing will cost a little more. They will normally quote you per A4 page or per 100 words: check whether this includes VAT or not.

These bureaux will often run a photocopying and document binding service, which will enhance the presentation of your work. This is important if you want to make a good impression on someone like your bank manager – it shows you mean business.

The bigger bureaux will be able to produce what is known as camera-ready copy (CRC) for something you want printed: this means that you do not have to pay the printer for making plates. The bureau will do this using something like desktop publishing (DTP) and a laser printer, which gives excellent quality output in a variety of styles and typefaces.

Solicitors

Lawyers have a reputation for being slow. This is because they have to protect your interests and their own by being extremely thorough about every word they draft. A badly-drawn document can cause untold misery. They also often have to deal with official bodies, such as local authorities, who are themselves slow to respond. If you need very quick action, make this clear to your solicitor; they *can* get things done very fast if necessary.

Solicitors often specialise in certain aspects of their work, such as litigation (court work) or housing. However, most firms will deal with basic legal work such as conveyancing, drawing up a lease, and so on.

A solicitor will advise you and draw up the appropriate documents for:

- Conveyancing
- Leasing
- Sub-letting
- Rental agreements (for the rental/hire of plant, machinery etc.)
- Planning permission
- A partnership agreement
- Employment law
  and more

There may be a Law Centre in your area which, if it cannot deal with your particular requirement, will advise you where to go to get the most cost-effective advice.

Solicitors should be able to give you a fairly accurate quotation for the work involved. Ask for this, so that you can budget accordingly.

CHAPTER **9** CHECKLIST

Most of the professionals listed in this chapter are needed only occasionally. Your accountant and bank manager are important to you – choose them with care. The services they can offer are, among others:

1 Accountant
  - Book-keeping
  - VAT returns
  - Annual trading accounts
  - Tax returns

2 Architects
  - Property surveys
  - Plans for planning permission

3 Banks
  - Current account with cash card
  - Deposit account
  - Standing orders
  - Direct debit
  - Credit transfers
  - Monthly statements
  - Loans
  - Overdrafts

4 Building societies
- Personal account services

5 Estate agents
- Property availability
- Local developments
- Planning and use restrictions
- Inventories

6 HM Customs and Excise (VAT)
- Making VAT returns
- What is and is not VATable

7 Insurance brokers
- Type of insurance you need
- The best policy or policies for you

8 Printers
- Printed stationery
- Advice on paper, letterheads etc.

9 Secretarial services
- Word processing
- Photocopying
- Binding

10 Solicitors
- Conveyancing
- Leasing and renting
- Planning permission
- Partnership agreement
- Memorandum and Articles of Association

10

The Office

In this Chapter

Stationery

Business documents
  Estimate; Quotation;
  Order; Invoice; Credit
  note; Statement;
  Remittance advice; Letters

Computers or not?
  Hardware; Software;
  Materials; Suppliers
Telecommunications *Tele-*
  phones; Fax; Telex, Tele-
  tex and Electronic Mail
Furniture and equipment
Health and safety at work
  act

Whatever your business, you need an 'office', even if it is only the corner of your dining table. You have to plan ahead to make sure you do not suddenly find you want to write a letter or send an invoice and you have no headed paper. You need to be systematic to keep your paperwork up to date.

Stationery

The stationery you are likely to need, depending on the nature of your business, is:

Headed paper for letters (at least 70 gsm, preferably 80 gsm in weight); gsm stands for grams per square metre

Plain paper   of the same weight and colour for continuation sheets

Unless you run a cash payment business

Paper   for Invoices   you can use your letterheads for all these, provided you give your document a definite name

Estimates

Quotations

If you have a personal computer, you may need any or all of this paper on continuous stationery.

Envelopes   Some good quality, the same weight and colour as your best paper, some manilla or white for run-of-the-mill correspondence

Labels   These are very useful for mail shots or for some computer printers which cannot take thick envelopes

Compliments Slips   These are merely a piece of your good paper with *With compliments* and your company name and address printed on. They are very useful for slipping in with the odd bit of advertising material or invoice; you do not have to bother to type a letter, but you can handwrite a short message

---

NEWCO

22 Elmhurst Road   Hawton   Northants   NN7 4PX

Telephone: 0327 63418   VAT Registration: 987 6543 21

With Compliments

Business cards	Have some of these done early, and have them with you at all times
Order Book/Bills	Your business might require standard books of order forms or bills with carbon interleaved: these can be useful until you get your printed Order Forms and Invoices organised

You will need to think about the design of your stationery. Try to get it to match your company image – and colours, if you have any. It is worth getting some expert advice on this: printers have a wide experience of styles and colours and can be really helpful. However, you have to be careful that printers do not get carried away with their own enthusiasm and run you up very large bills. Some well-established printers prefer to do longer runs and charge a lot for very small orders. Some printers specialise in short runs – these are the ones you should try to seek out. Franchises such as Prontaprint or Mister Print can be a good place to start – they sometimes do a 'starter pack' just to get you under way. (See Chapter 9.)

If you can get a good master copy of your letterhead made, you can get the first batch of stationery (100–200 sheets) copied on a good photocopier provided you are happy to have your letterhead in black. Make a master with your letterhead on it, and photocopy this onto your (coloured) quality paper. This is the sort of run that a professional printer will not want to bother with, and for which you could be charged more than is necessary. As soon as your style, address and amounts required are established, you can shop around and get all your printing requirements professionally produced.

Things to remember to put on your letterheads:

- Company logo (if any)
- Company name, address and telephone number
- Telex and fax numbers (if any)
- VAT registration number (if any)
- Names of proprietor, partners or directors (See Chapter 4)

It is very important to keep copies of all your business documents. If you are using a typewriter, you can use flimsy paper (bank) and carbon paper; if you are using a word processor or personal computer, you can do a rough printout of your document to check that it is right, or a photocopy of the finished product. A box of scrap paper (all the printouts you reject or the unused sides of junk mail) is useful for rough printouts. You can save reams that way. It may seem fussy, but you can lose a lot of your profit in wastage if you do not order and use your stationery economically, without sacrificing the excellence of your image.

All business stationery and printing can be charged to the business, and the VAT is reclaimable. (See Chapter 7.)

Stationery suppliers

You can get supplies of stationery from High Street shops, but a stationery supplier is often more economical. You will find these in Yellow Pages or your local Thomsons Directory. What suppliers often do is use a standard catalogue and fix their own prices; they sometimes have special offers on standard stationery such as photo-copying paper, envelopes, typewriter or printer ribbons etc. There can be an enormous difference in price, delivery facilities and payment terms, so it is worth shopping around.

As a business, you can also use a cash and carry wholesaler like Nurdin & Peacock or Makro, but of course they do not deliver. However, they are usually open till late at night and sometimes seven days a week. You might already be intending to buy from a cash and carry wholesaler, particularly if you run a small retail shop. If so, remember the office side (in the non-foods area) as well.

Business documents

When you are laying out your business documents, make sure that each has all the information needed and, most important, the right name of the document. Call an Estimate a Quotation, and you could land yourself in trouble. Always remember to include your company name, address and telephone number on every document.

Different types of business need different documents, but here are descriptions and formats for the main ones. Look at the design and layout of the documents coming in to your business; this will help with the layout and design of your own.

Estimate
(ordinary headed paper will do)

This is an *estimate*, as it says, of how much the service will cost. An

NEWCO

22 Elmhurst Road   Hawton   Northants   NN7 4PX

Telephone: 0327 63418

VAT Registration: 987 6543 21

ESTIMATE

(Today's date)

Mr R V Pugh
12 Ravens Close
Willington
Northants
NN7 6RL

Estimate for redecorating outside of
'Mountside' Hill Lane Andley

To: re-paint the windows, doors and
      garden gate on the outside of the
      property in a colour to be
      selected.

                    for the sum of   <u>£660</u>
                         plus VAT

Please note:

If our estimate is accepted, work will be started in
one month's time.

estimate is not necessarily the final price to be charged. It is often used by businesses like builders and decorators which do not know what they might uncover.

Remember to say that VAT is extra – for instance *All charges subject to x% VAT E & O E* (Errors and Omissions Excepted) is often added at the bottom.

Quotation
(ordinary headed paper)
A quotation gives a firm price for a product or service, again usually net of VAT. The layout can be the same as for an Estimate.

Order
(printed or typed format needed)
If you need your customers to place written orders for your product or service, you can provide them with an Order Form. This will make sure that you get all the details *you* need to fulfil the order correctly. Do not forget VAT, postage and packing or carriage and discounts, if these are applicable.

Invoice
(printed format desirable, but can be typed on headed paper)
These are the details which should always appear on an Invoice:

1   Name and address of supplier
2   Name and address of purchaser/customer
3   Date
4   Invoice Number
5   Order Number (if applicable) or Reference
6   Quantity and description of goods (plus catalogue number if applicable) or service
7   Unit price
8   Total without VAT
9   Discount (if applicable)
10 Postage and packing, carriage (if applicable)
11 Final net total
12 Amount of VAT at appropriate percentage(s)
13 Total including VAT
14 VAT registration number
15 Payment terms

NEWCO

22 Elmhurst Road   Hawton   Northants   NN7 4PX
Telephone: 0327 63418   VAT Registration: 987 6543 21

ORDER

Date (Today's date)
Order No 52879
To Paper Supplies Ltd
        78 Church Road
        DARTFORD
        Kent
        DA12 6TU

QTY	DESCRIPTION	UNIT PRICE	£ PRICE
10	Boxes white photocopy paper	12.00	120.00
5	Reams blue photocopy paper	2.90	14.50
20	Courier 10 plastic daisy wheels	3.75	75.00
50	Diablo 101 carbon ribbons	1.60	80.00

Net	289.50
VAT 15%	43.42
Grand Total	332.92

① **NEWCO**

22 Elmhurst Road   Hawton   Northants   NN7 4PX
Telephone: 0327 63418   ⑭ VAT Registration: 987 6543 21

INVOICE

③ **Date:** (Today's date)   ④ **Invoice No:** 2101

⑤ **Order No:** 365

② **To:** Messrs P J Voyce and Partners
            213 High Road
            BURNLEY
            Lancs BB1 2VW

DESCRIPTION	PRICE £
⑥ 40 copies Contract ⑦ @ £2.00 each Preliminaries	80.00
2 copies Final Contract @ £13.00 each	26.00
⑧ NET VALUE	106.00
⑨ LESS DISCOUNT AT 2.5%	2.65
	103.35
⑩ PLUS CARRIAGE	10.00
	⑪ 113.35
⑫ VAT AT 15%	17.00
⑬ INVOICE TOTAL	£130.35

⑮ Terms 30 days net

Credit Note
(printing and layout similar to an Invoice)
Sometimes if an Order has not been totally fulfilled, the goods are unsatisfactory or a client has overpaid for some reason, you have to issue a Credit Note, stating the amount and the reason. Try to relate the Credit Note to your Order Number or Invoice Number – and remember to allow the customer the credit due on the next Invoice or Statement.

Statement
(printed form desirable, but can be done on headed paper)
Occasionally you have to render a Statement of a customer's account – it is often a reminder to pay. Some companies make it a policy to pay only on receipt of a Statement. If, through experience, you find out that a company adopts this policy, you should render the Statement almost simultaneously with the Invoice. Some companies render a document which they call an Invoice/Statement, and some send out Statements of Account automatically every month.

The Statement should show the dates and numbers of outstanding Invoices and details of totals without and with VAT. Details of the products or services need not be included – you have already given this information on the Invoices. Some Statements include the length of time the Invoices have been outstanding, and any payments received during the Statement period. Remember to date the Statement.

Remittance Advice
(probably printed, attached to Invoice or Statement)
When your customers pay you, it is useful for you if they fill in your own Remittance Advice (some companies make this a tear-off slip on the Invoice or Statement). Rather like the Order, it gives you details which make the book-keeping easier at your end – the details on the Remittance Advice will be of your choosing, and may include your name, address and customer reference number, your customer's name and address, Invoice Number date and totals without and with VAT.

The secret of all these documents is to have as few variables on each as possible – all you should have to do when sending the

NEWCO

22 Elmhurst Road   Hawton   Northants   N7 4PX
Telephone: 0327 63418

VAT Registration: 987 6543 21

STATEMENT

Statement date: (Today's date)

To: Messrs P J Voyce and Partners
213 High Road
BURNLEY
Lancs BB1 2VW

Invoice date	Invoice number	DEBIT £	CREDIT £	Balance due £
(Date of Invoice)	2101	130.35		130.35

document out is to fill in details relevant to that particular customer. You should not have to fill in document name, your own company name and details, for instance, every time. Use a computer, or get the documents printed.

Letters

It is very important for your image to send out letters which are correctly typed and spelled and look good on the page. If it is a short letter, leave plenty of margin space all round.

Try to address your letters to a named person or a job title, if you are writing to a company ('The Sales Director', for example). Letters addressed to the company only tend to get shunted round from department to department. Identify quickly what you are writing about by giving either a reference, or a heading, or both.

A typical business letter layout is shown on page 102.

If you are in any doubt about your spelling, grammar or sentence construction, get someone to check it for you. All your documentation should be to the high standard you set yourself for the rest of your business operation.

If you are not used to office work – how to address people, sizes and weights of stationery, basic spelling and grammar, you would find *Teach Yourself Secretary's Handbook* by Vera and Christina Hughes useful. Alternatively use the services of a Secretarial Bureau (See Chapter 9).

Computers or not?

If you think you can cope well with your own office work, and are used to using a typewriter, you will find a small personal computer very useful. It will take you quite a bit of time to learn how to use it, if you have not used one before, but in the end, for you or the person who is doing your office work, it will make a lot of difference. It might not save an expert typist a lot of time, but it will make the quality of the output – your letters, invoices and so on – so much better. If, however, you have no idea about keyboards, document layout and so on, it might be better to postpone buying a computer until your business is well underway. If you are a complete novice, learning to use a personal computer can be a very lengthy process; it can also be extremely frustrating. In the very early stages of your

NEWCO

22 Elmhurst Road   Hawton   Northants   NN7 4PX
Telephone: 0327 63418   V.A.T Registration: 987 6543 21

(Today's Date)

Mr D Waverley
Customer Relations Manager
B & A Pyecroft Ltd
16 Southampton Row
LONDON
SE14 4ZW

Dear Mr Waverley

THERMAL BINDING

We are pleased to announce a new service which we think
will improve the presentation of your work and enhance your
company image. Your important documents can now be
thermal bound in plain, transparent or window covers in an
attractive range of colours.

   For real impact and style your company name and logo
   can be printed on the covers. The printing can be done
   in black, blue or gold; choose the colour which best
   suits the cover.

Please read our enclosed leaflet, which we are sure you will
find exciting. It contains not only a list of our charges, but
also illustrations of how your documents could look. It gives
full details of colours, sizes and styles, and our attractive
introductory offer on prices.
Try our new THERMAL BINDING service and present your
documents with pride.

Yours sincerely

Ala Na

Office Manager

Enc

business, it is probably better to devote your time and energy to providing the actual product or service. Someone has to do the office work, and you need to decide which is the best method of tackling this.

What will you get in a personal computer package, and what can you use it for? You should get:

Hardware: a keyboard, screen, disk drive and printer as well as the central processing unit (CPU) which makes the whole thing work.

The keyboard will be a normal QWERTY keyboard – so called because those are the first letters of the alpha keys on the top row – with extra function keys. Some will have a numeric keypad on the right, but you can always use the numbers on the top row of the keyboard proper. Remember to use the $\emptyset$, not a capital 'O', for nought and a 1, not a small 'l' (ell), for one.

The screen will probably present no problems, but there are various colours (white on black, green on black, black on white, yellow on brown, etc.) and various flicker rates. Ask the supplier about these, particularly if you suffer from epilepsy. Choose a screen to suit yourself.

The disk drive will probably be an integral part of the whole terminal. Make sure the system has the facility for copying work onto backup disks – it is essential to take backup copies of really important information.

The printer is the key to the quality of output. Get as good a printer as you can afford. You can probably choose from dot matrix (make sure it will do NLQ (near letter quality) printing), daisy wheel or laser. The last is the best and most expensive. You can get quite reasonable results from a good dot matrix, but they are slow compared with the others, and not as versatile as daisy wheel printers.

The software: the computer programs, which allow you to do things such as word processing, book-keeping and so on. You do not need to be able to write computer programs to operate a computer.

You could get (in descending order of priority):

(a) A good word processing package, for correspondence, reports etc.

(b) An accounts package for book-keeping

(c) A spreadsheet, which you can use for doing cash flow forecasts production forecasts, etc.

(d) A spellchecker for checking your spelling; they are not infallible because they often cannot cope with homonyms (their/ there etc.) – this often comes as part of the WP package

(e) A desk-top publishing package. This is a program which, combined with a laser printer, will give your documents that really printed look. It can get the printer to do all sorts of printstyles, borders and graphics. However, versatile desk-top publishing packages are as yet fairly complicated and most are not for the beginner. They can also be expensive, partly because of the printer required. There are some software programs which are something between an ordinary word processing package and a full desk-top publishing program, and these can be worthwhile if you really need your 'printed' material to look good. If you are a real beginner, though, it is probably better to start with a simple WP package.

Sometimes some or all of these software packages are included with the hardware package you buy, but sometimes they come as extras. You need to check.

You always get at least one instruction manual *but* some are still incomprehensible to non-computer people. Sometimes you find word processing instructions which are 'idiot-proof' and accounting instructions which you cannot understand, all in the same manual. Again you need to check.

The materials
As well as the system (hardware and software) you will need:

Cables	sometimes part of the package, sometimes extra
Disks	as well as disks which make your PC work (called system, operator or program disks), which will probably come with the PC package, you will need disks on which to store the work you do. Some system disks have a lot of storage space on them, and you will not need extra disks at first
Ribbons	for daisy wheel or dot matrix printers

Printwheels	for daisy wheel printers. Some are metal, some plastic. The plastic are a lot cheaper, so you can buy a variety, and they will last reasonably well if looked after
Paper	and possibly a hopper or tractor feed to feed the paper into the printer

There are lots of other 'extras' which you may or may not need. Look at a computer supplies catalogue if you want to see the sort of thing you can get. Remember anyway that you have to budget for at least the basics, which can cost quite a bit in both money and learning time.

Computer suppliers
As with stationery, you can buy a PC in many High Street shops, but it is worth going to a supplier who can advise you on what is best for you, and give you help when you need it initially. Computer manufacturers will usually be able to give you the name of your nearest supplier of their machines, and adverts for the packages are in almost every newspaper.

Take time to do some research before laying out capital on a PC, because it is a significant cost in your opening budget. Visiting a PC, computer or micro exhibition can be helpful, but try to go with someone who knows what to look for.

You might like to consider having a maintenance agreement for any of the larger systems. It is something to talk to your supplier about, because you become very machine dependent and can lose a lot of business if your system stops working for any length of time.

Telecommunications

This is the word for any method of computerised communication between businesses, and includes telephones, fax, telex, electronic mail, computer networks and so on. We shall deal only with telephones, telex, fax and electronic mail, although to begin with the telephone will probably be your sole method of communication.

Telephones
Obviously you will need a telephone, but will an ordinary telephone be enough? These are the alternative extras you could consider:

- Plug-in extensions or small, modern PBX (private branch exchange) – which used to be known as the switchboard
- Last number re-dial (press a button and the last number you dialled is automatically re-dialled)
- Loudspeaker and mike, so you do not have to use the handset, and everyone in the office can hear what is being said, and can join in
- Memory for those numbers you use frequently
- Car phone: prestigious, but is it essential?
  It might be an essential part of your communications plan; it depends on how necessary it is to be able to get hold of you at all times. It might also ease family tensions if you can let the people at home know how late you will be
- Answering machine: this can be an integral part of the telephone terminal. It is useful to have one where you can pick up your messages from a distance, either voice or gadget activated. If you are offering a service, and the office is not always manned, we consider an answering machine to be essential

Fax

This is short for facsimile; facsimile copies of documents can be transmitted almost anywhere in the world. The document is fed into the transmitting machine and sent via the telephone lines to the receiving fax machine. Machines are required at both ends of the communication channel, linked by a telephone line. Fax is becoming very widely used; if your business is concerned with sending copies of documents to a large number of customers, a Fax machine could be your next bit of telecommunications hardware after your telephone and answering machine.

Some machines incorporate Fax, telephone, copier and answering machine all in one small unit, which means only one telephone line is needed. This could be ideal for the very small business.

Telex, Teletex and Electronic Mail

Telex is a system run by British Telecom which allows you to communicate in text with any other Telex user in the world via a telephone line. You have to rent or buy the Telex machine yourself, which for a very small business can be quite expensive. Telex can only carry messages in capital letters and is fairly slow, but Teletex (a development of Telex) allows you to transmit messages in small and capital letters, and is faster and more expensive to install.

Electronic Mail (usually called Email) transmits messages from one computer to another, again via the telephone lines. You need an Email software package on your computer. The sender dials a central number and transmits to the receiver's mailbox. Email is faster and cheaper than telex, but:

- both sender and receiver have to belong to the same Email service
- Telex automatically prints out at the receiver's end. Email users have to dial into their mailbox to see if there are any messages, and they frequently forget to do so

It is possible to send Email to Telex users, and vice versa. Both Telex and Email use text only and can send and receive messages at any hour of the day or night. For graphs, drawings or photographs you would have to communicate by fax.

There are several competing Email services which, as yet, will not allow you to communicate between networks. This should change within the next few years. The market leader is Telecom Gold; other Email services are Mercury Link 7500, One-to-one and Datalink. The checklist on page 113 gives telephone numbers.

If you have customers who are widely scattered, and to whom you need to send text messages (as opposed to telephone or fax) it could be worth your while to have an Email facility on your personal computer so that you can communicate with Telex and other Email users quickly and at any time of day.

Furniture and equipment

Furniture

You can manage with very little purpose-built furniture to start with, but you should try to keep all your business documentation separate from your general household paperwork, if you are working from home.

You will find that you very soon need, at least:

- Files in which to keep correspondence, copy invoices, etc.
- Somewhere to keep the files – probably a two-drawer cabinet will do to start with

108

- Somewhere to store your stationery – desk drawers or a small cupboard are better than filing cabinet drawers
- A table or desk for your typewriter or personal computer – make sure it is big enough to take the typewriter/PC *and* the papers you are working from
- A chair of the right height for writing or typing. It may not be you who does the writing or typing, but whoever does it needs a desk or table and chair of the right height. This is very important, because working for any length of time at the wrong height can cause backache, wristache and all sorts of other aches and pains. It is worth getting an adjustable typing chair with good back support

There is usually a second-hand office furniture shop not too far away, from which you can get your basic furniture. Sometimes you can be lucky and hear of a large office which is being refurbished and needs to get rid of its out-of-date furniture. This can be quite prestigious furniture, but if you are working from home, make sure it will fit in! If your business requires prestigious looking furniture from the start, remember to include the cost in your business plan.

Equipment
Items of equipment you may need are:

Stapler and staples
Hole puncher
Guillotine
Paper clips
Liquid eraser (Tippex)
Metal waste paper bin
Franking machine, if your business requires lots of mail shots
Sellotape
Scissors

Desk lamp(s): it is important to have good direct lighting on your papers, particularly if you are working with a PC – light reflecting on the screen can give you eyestrain
Fireproof and smokeproof container for very important reference sources, like accounts books, and computer disks
A safe to keep money and valuable items, if yours is a retail business

FRANKING MACHINE
If your postal output is sufficient to warrant it, you could use a

franking machine. If you are a franking machine user, you have to:

- obtain authority from the local Head Post Office before starting to use a machine
- pay in advance for postage at a specified post office
- follow the local conditions about how to face and bundle franked mail (ask the local Head Postmaster)
- return a completed control card to the Post Office at the close of business each working week
- use a machine authorised by the Post Office and have it regularly maintained. Authorised suppliers are listed in the Post Office Guide

PHOTOCOPIER

After a telephone and typewriter or PC, a good photocopier is probably the next most important item of equipment. Get as good a one as you can afford. These are some of the features to look out for:

- Automatic sheet feed
- Double-sided copying
- Collator
- Reduction and enlargement
- Memory for reduction and enlargement
- Two-page separation, for copying pages of books or magazines (but watch the copyright laws) and A3 masters as two separate A4 sheets

Large suppliers are always willing to lease you a photocopier, with integrated Maintenance Agreement. This can be advantageous from the accounting point of view (ask your accountant) and very import-ant if your copier is going to get heavy wear – it is the one item of office equipment which always seems to be jamming or breaking down. If you lease, you have to remember that you pay a charge every time you press the button, as well as your quarterly leasing bill.

If you buy your copier outright, you have no leasing charges, but you might spend a lot in maintenance. It is possible to get a Maintenance Agreement for copiers which are owned – ask the manufacturers how to go about this. There is a second-hand market in photocopiers, but you usually do not know how they have been used or misused.

There are plenty of photocopier paper suppliers around, but if you use inferior paper you can find it never stops jamming, or takes through two sheets at a time. It is worth considering using the paper sold, or at least recommended, by the suppliers.

HASAWA

Many people forget that HASAWA (The Health and Safety at Work Act) applies just as much in the office as it does in any other workplace. If you are on your own, health and safety in the office is important because you cannot afford to have accidents. If you are employing others, you have a legal obligation to make their working conditions healthy and safe.

Health and Safety in the office is really common sense, but here are a few DOS and DON'TS

DO
- Make sure the electrical wiring is in good condition
- Route wires and cables through conduit
- Have the right fire extinguishers handy and topped up – and know how to use them
- Have sensible arrangements for making hot drinks
- Observe the precautions for unjamming paper in the photocopier – some parts of the machine get very hot
- Lift heavy items (e.g. boxes of paper) properly
- Keep fire exits clear at all times
- Know what to do in the event of a fire
- Ensure any staff know the fire drill
- Have the first aid box in a handy place

DON'T
- Leave cabinet and cupboard doors open
- Open more than one drawer of a filing cabinet at a time
- Leave cables trailing
- Leave piles of papers and files where people can trip over them
- Let jewellery and ties or scarves dangle in moving parts of equipment – e.g. printers
- Carry things which are too heavy for you (e.g. electric typewriters); get help, or use a trolley

- Stand on chairs – use steps
- Use adhesive sprays (like Spray Mount) in confined spaces without ventilation
- Smoke

What about VDUs?

People fear that prolonged use of VDUs will cause many aches, pains and even permanent damage. There are various *Health and Safety Executive* publications on this issue, giving the latest research findings, advice and guidance. Write to: Health and Safety Executive, Regina House, Old Marylebone Road, London NW1.

PREGNANCY

There is a fear of birth abnormalities, but there is no firm evidence that VDUs are a health hazard to pregnant women. Radiation from VDUs (the equivalent to that from a hair dryer or an electric blanket) does *not* appear to be a cause of birth abnormalities.

Stress through fear of working with VDUs can cause problems, as can badly-designed work stations. If you are pregnant and worried about working with VDUs, try and arrange for someone else to do so. If a member of your staff is similarly concerned, treat the matter sympathetically and make alternative arrangements.

EYESTRAIN

People do complain of eyestrain and headaches after prolonged use of VDUs, but there is no evidence that VDU use damages the eyes. It is much more likely that spectacles are not worn when they are needed, or that incorrect spectacles are worn (bi-focals can be a particular problem), or that workstation design and job content is at fault. If in any doubt at all:

- have your eyes tested by an optician who knows about VDUs
- check the workstation design, particularly for glare
- consider the job rotation and whether you are spending too long at the VDU without a break. VDU work is very concentrated, which in itself can cause stress and fatigue

DESIGN OF WORKSTATIONS

Badly-designed workstations are the most likely cause of aches and pains. Check the following:

- Sufficient space on the worktop, with document holders if required
- The worktop is at the right height
- The printer is at the right height
- The chair is comfortable and adjustable for height and angle
- Lighting is sufficient to illuminate surfaces from which work is being copied
- Lighting should not be directed straight onto the screen whether it is sunlight or artificial light – it can cause glare
- Ambient lighting should not be too harsh
- Daylight needs extra directional lighting for dull days and blinds for very sunny days
- A comfortable working temperature is required
- Use anti-static mats, sprays, etc. if necessary
- A pleasing decor is helpful – if working towards a wall, make sure you look at something unobtrusive and restful
- Do not work facing a window
- Make sure you sit up straight with your back supported and with your hands at the right angle to the keyboard
- Adjust the brightness of the screen to suit your requirements.

In general

There is a lot of work involved in setting up the admin and office side of your business, which can sometimes seem like time ill spent. You cannot run an efficient business without a good administrative backup – for instance, it is no good selling the product or service if you cannot collect the money – so do not begrudge the time spent on getting the office setup right from the start.

If you are opening a shop, your office requirements, from the cash handling point of view, will be different; turn to Chapter 12.

CHAPTER **10** CHECKLIST
1   Design logo
2   Get letterheads designed and artwork done
3   Organise preliminary supply of stationery
4   Design documentation – invoices, order forms etc.
5   Decide on typing method – typewriter or PC?
6   Organise telephones and answering machine
7   Get basic furniture

8 Organise preliminary filing system

9 Decide on photocopying method – own, buy, lease or outside

10 Get essential items of equipment (see list on page 108)

11 Check layout of office for ease of working and safety

Useful telephone numbers for Email services: Telecom Gold – 071 403 6777; Mercury Link 7500 – 081 847 6070; One-to-One – 071 351 2468; Datalink – 0532 442219.

Telephone number for the Health and Safety Executive: 071 723 1262.

11

Employing Others

In this Chapter

Staff recruitment
  *Advertising; Selection and
  interviewing*
Pay *Methods and
  frequency of payment;
  National Insurance, tax
  and SSP; Maternity rights
  and pay; Pensions, holiday
  pay and sick pay*
Contract of employment
  *Main requirements;
  Disciplinary procedure
  and periods of notice*

Insurance
HASAWA *Employer's
  obligations and policy
  statement; Accident book;
  First aid*
Data Protection Act *Do
  you need to register?; An
  employee's rights*
Staff training *Induction
  training; Further training*

It is quite a big step to start employing other people when you have been running a business on your own or in partnership. Employing others is not nearly such a minefield as many fear, however. For one thing, it is not true to say that you cannot get rid of an employee who turns out to be totally unreliable or incompetent – you can.

If you set out to be a reasonable, fair and sensible employer, and follow the basic rules about employing others, you have nothing to fear. There are plenty of sources of advice on the law and your statutory obligations: these will be mentioned in this chapter.

NB The rules and basics on employment law are given as they stand in 1989/90. Please bear in mind that some may alter between now and 1992, when it is the goal that all employees in the European Community shall have common conditions of employment.

Staff recruitment

The first person you employ is often a friend or a member of the family. How do you set about finding someone you do not know, and selecting the right person to suit you and your method of working?

Advertising

When advertising in the local press or the Job Centre, remember to include in the advertisement at least: job title; location; pay; full- or part-time; any special skills required; how to apply.

Your advertisement must not discriminate on grounds of race or sex, or whether a person is married, single, and so on; you may put preferred ages. It is illegal to employ children under 13; children between 13 and school leaving age may be employed under certain conditions; they can be employed to do a paper round, for example. There is no upper age limit for employment, and with the abolition of the earnings rule, pensioners may now earn as much as they wish. Mature people often make very good employees, especially on a part-time basis.

Croner's *Reference Book for Employers*, published by Croner Publishers Ltd, Croner House, 173 Kingston Road, New Malden, Surrey KT3 3SS, gives full details of this and many other aspects of employing other people. It runs an updating service so that you receive updates whenever the law changes.

Use your advertisement to sift replies, if you have several, so that you interview only possible candidates. Reply to all those who apply, even if it is only to say no.

Selection

To make sure you get the right person for the job, you must know what you are looking for. It is advisable to draw up a Job

Specification (this is not a Job Description, which is described later in this chapter – page 117).

A Job Specification lists those elements which are *essential* in the person you want to employ, and those which are *desirable*. It could look something like this:

Job Specification

Job title:	WP Operator/clerk	
	Essential	Desirable
Qualifications:		
	'O' level Maths/English or equivalent	
	Good with figures	
	WP Exam	
	Good telephone technique	Experience of book-keeping
Age:		30–50
Travel:	Lives near	Driving licence
Special:	Must be prepared to work without supervision	

This employer is obviously looking for someone to run a small office. If you think that 'good with figures' and 'good telephone technique' are essential, you should have some way of testing this. As far as the telephone techniques are concerned, you could get applicants to telephone for an application form and make notes of how they deal with you on the phone. 'Good with figures' sometimes requires a simple maths test – 'O' level Maths is not always a sufficient indicator. 'O' level English does not mean that someone is capable of writing a good, clear, business English letter.

You can learn quite a lot from the way people fill in an application form, so try to use one. The areas normally covered in an application for employment form are: name; address; date of birth; qualifications; employment history; outside interests. Some forms include nationality; present age; educational history and family background (children, for instance).

Ask applicants to complete the form in their own handwriting, so you can see whether they can write neatly, can spell correctly and so on, if this is important to the job. The previous work experience can also be very revealing: it can give you a good idea of whether a prospective employee can hold down a job for a sensible length of time, or whether he or she tends to flit from job to job. Explore any gaps (even of a few months) in the working history. It could be that the applicant has been in prison. This is not a good reason for rejecting an applicant out-of-hand, but you need to know. Look out for any discrepancies in the way the form has been completed – for example, does the stated age tie up with the date of birth? If people are less than truthful on an application form, they might be slightly less than honest in their employment. If you ask for 'hobbies' on the form, explore what applicants mean by their replies. For example, 'football': does this mean they play (in which case they are probably fit) or do they watch? For 'music', if they listen, that is different from playing an instrument, which requires perseverance and manipulative skills. If they play in a group, band or orchestra, it shows you they are used to working with others.

From the application forms, select perhaps three or four to interview. Reject at once any which do not fulfil the *essential* requirements. Ask the applicants questions to get them talking about themselves, their home circumstances, why they want the job. Of course you should also make sure they understand not only what the terms and conditions of employment are, but also what the job entails. Write out a Job Description or a Schedule of Duties. For a WP Operator/clerk it could look something like this:

Schedule of Duties
Job title: WP Operator/clerk

1 Deal with all incoming and outgoing mail
2 Answer the telephone
3 Write letters
4 Do the company's book-keeping
5 Pay wages
6 Undertake banking
7 Use the Fax machine
8 Any other job needed to keep the office running smoothly

This is simply a statement of the duties to be performed. A Job Description would probably set out what the overall purpose of the job is, to whom the job holder is responsible and the standards required for each duty listed.

If you let prospective employees see at least a Schedule of Duties at the interview stage (or send one with the Application Form) they can decide whether they can cope with the job, and might weed themselves out at an early stage. If you discuss the Schedule at the interview stage, it will give you an opportunity to find out where any weaknesses lie and where training would be needed. The last duty 'Any other job' is vague, but it does mean the employees, if they accept the job based on the Schedule of Duties, agree to be flexible. Make sure that you make no handwritten comments on the application form which could in any way be described as discriminating – it is illegal.

Use the interview fully so that each side can find out as much as possible about each other. It takes time, but it is time well invested. A good employee will stay with you and quickly become part of the company. Employees who do not fit in leave, and then you have to start all over again.

Once you have made your selection, made a formal job offer in writing to the successful applicant, and have had a definite acceptance in writing, write to those who were not successful.

Pay

The amount of gross pay, plus overtime rates if applicable, will have been agreed between you at the interview/job offer stage. It is also useful to agree at that early stage:

- the method of payment (straight into bank account or building society by credit transfer, cheque or cash)
- the frequency of payment (weekly or monthly)

From an employer's point of view it is much less of a security risk to pay straight into an account by credit transfer. It is also more economical to pay monthly rather than weekly, because you usually pay in arrears, so you have the use of that money for about three weeks. An employee might wish to be paid weekly in cash. You, as the employer, must make up your mind what you are prepared to do and stick to it. You cannot force an employee to change once (s)he has started work, but you can lay down conditions of employment at the start.

As an employer you are committed to pay the employee the amounts and on the terms agreed. You must pay this, no matter what state the business is in.

You also have to make statutory deductions from the gross pay. These are:

- Income Tax
- National Insurance – employee's contribution
  The employer's contribution is paid over and above the agreed wage of the employee, and is a percentage of that figure

For all details of deductions, how they should be collected and how and when paid to the authorities, tax tables and so on, ask the DSS and the Inland Revenue. ACAS also do a very helpful leaflet called *Employing People in the Small Business*. You can get this from the Job Centre.

You must supply the employee with the following:

- Detailed wage/salary slip showing the gross pay, all the deductions and the net amount payable. It does not matter if this slip is handwritten, but it must be given with the pay
- An annual P60 showing the amount of tax deducted in that financial year. This is the government's financial year from 5 April to 4 April, not the company's financial year
- If the employee leaves your employment, a P45 showing the amount of tax deducted to date in that financial year

Statutory Sick Pay (SSP)
As an employer, if your employee falls sick and is away from work for four days or more, you must pay the employee sick pay, instead of a wage, on behalf of the government. You are entitled to claim this money back from the DSS in the form of a deduction from the National Insurance you have to pay. There are strict rules about how much must be paid, when and to whom, and about doctors' certificates. Ask your local DSS for details and for help if you are having to do this for the first time.

Maternity rights and pay
A pregnant woman has three statutory rights:

1 Time off with pay for ante-natal care: she does not need to have worked for you for a specific length of time
2 Maternity pay if she has worked for you for at least 26 weeks up to the 15th week before the expected week of confinement (EWC) *and* earns more than £35 per week
3 The right to return to work after maternity leave if she wishes and gives the requisite notice

There are rules about what constitutes 'ante-natal care', how much notice the woman must give her employer, how much she is entitled to be paid and what an employer must do about keeping her job for her. Ask the DSS for details on all these points.

Pensions, holiday pay and sick pay

These have been lumped together under one heading, because the employer has no statutory obligations under these headings except those mentioned above (NI deductions and SSP).

An employer is not obliged to run a company pension scheme or a sick pay scheme. A sick pay scheme is one in which the employer pays an employee probably a full wage for a certain number of weeks off sick in a year, reducing the amount the longer the employee is away from work: the amount, for quite a long time, is normally higher than the employee would get from the government.

An employer is not obliged to grant anyone paid holiday – indeed, as the law currently stands, an employer is not obliged to grant an employee any holiday at all, except the statutory holidays (Christmas Day, Bank holidays).

Contracts of employment

An employer is obliged, within 13 weeks of an employee starting the job, to give an employee a written Contract of Employment. There should be two copies of the Contract, signed by both parties – one copy to each.

The Contract should include:

1 Names of parties
2 Job title
3 Hours of work

4 Rate of pay and how it is calculated (overtime, etc. if it is part of the basic pay, called 'built-in overtime')
5 When and how payable
6 Holiday entitlement and sick pay arrangements (if none, say so)
7 Pension arrangements, if any
8 Period of notice
9 Grievance procedures
10 Disciplinary procedures

The ACAS booklet *Employing Other People in the Small Business* sets all this out very clearly.

Dismissal

You can dismiss people for:

incompetence; misconduct; redundancy; special circumstances (for instance loss of driving licence if a driving licence is essential to the job); any other substantial reason

You can dismiss peopole who have up to six months' service with the company without a written statement. Between six months' and two years' service requires a written statement. After two years, you must have followed the full disciplinary procedures.

The disciplinary procedure is normally:

1 Verbal warning (noted in book)
2 Written warning
3 Final written warning

Instant dismissal for a grave offence, like proven theft, is legal. The point of the legislation is to ensure that people are not dismissed out-of-hand for no good reason. A good employer will always:

• investigate the circumstances
• tell the employee exactly what the problem is
• give the employee the chance (and the training, if necessary) to put the matter right

Provided you deal with your employees fairly, and with understanding, you should not fall foul of the law. It is worth documenting all that happens very carefully, in case you have to answer to an Industrial Tribunal.

Grievance procedure

This is really for companies who have a hierarchy of employees – managers, supervisors, operators and so on. It sets out to whom people can go if they have a genuine grievance – usually their immediate line manager, and one step above if this fails.

Period of notice

These are the *minimum* periods of notice an employer must give to an employee:

- Up to one month's service – none
- Between one month's and two years' service – one week
- After two years – one week's notice for each complete year of service until (s)he has more than twelve years' service, when the minimum notice period remains at twelve weeks

An employee can leave without notice during the first month of service. After that an employee has an obligation to give at least a week's notice. Longer periods are normally written into the Contract of Employment.

Redundancy

It is unlikely that you will get into a redundancy situation in the early years of the business. The point about redundancy is that, for some reason, the job no longer exists, and therefore you have to make someone redundant.

There are rules about redundancy and redundancy payments which you can obtain from the Department of Employment (start with the Job Centre).

Insurance

As well as insurance on buildings, contents, public liability and possibly professional negligence, as an employer you have to have Employer's Liability Insurance, and display the Insurance Certificate where employees can see it. Your Insurance Broker (see Chapter 9) should be able to advise you.

HASAWA

The Health and Safety at Work Act 1974 requires all employers, self-employed people and employees not to put themselves or anyone else (including contractors, for instance) at risk.

Employers have an additional responsibility to ensure that the working environment (including offices) will not be detrimental to the safety and health of employees, contractors and anyone else working on their premises. This includes safe systems, storage and machinery, as well as proper fire precautions and procedures.

Policy Statement

If you employ five people or more, you are obliged to draw up a Health and Safety Policy Statement, and display it where every employee can read it.

Accident Book

You are also obliged to keep a record of all accidents – normally in an Accident Book. An entry in the Accident Book must show:

- Name, sex, age, occupation of victim
- Nature of injury and place where it occurred
- Description of circumstances

For full details of regulations, see booklet HS(R)S. This can be obtained from the Health and Safety Executive. (For their address and telephone number see page 170.)

First aid

You do not need to have a qualified first aider on the premises until you have 150 or more employees. However, it is sensible, if possible, to have someone who can administer first aid.

At the very least you should have a First Aid box, easily accessible and regularly topped up. For details of what the box should contain, plus a full and clear description of what to do, see the *First Aid Manual*, published jointly by The British Red Cross Society, St John Ambulance Brigade and St Andrew's Ambulance Association, obtainable from book shops. A brief description of what to do is outlined in *Teach Yourself Secretary's Handbook* by Vera and Christina Hughes.

Data Protection Act

This Act applies to data held electronically (on computer, even if it is only a PC). It does not apply to handwritten or typed records.

If you have stored electronically any personal data about your employees beyond just names and addresses – for instance, if you have personnel information about rates of pay, domestic circumstances and so on, you must register as a data user with the Data Protection Registrar. The form DPR1 is available at main Post Offices.

Your employees have a right to know what personal data is being held, and whether it is correct. In practice, this means that most employers give their employees a printout of the information held once a year, and ask them to confirm or update it.

If you are using personal data purely for personnel reasons with your company you will have no problems. Problems arise when you use or disclose that data for some other purpose (selling employee lists to a marketing company, for example).

Here again, provided employers go about their business in a normal, straightforward and fair way, they should not fall foul of the law.

Staff training

Staff training is not necessarily about sending people away on courses, although this might be required sometimes. Staff training is about making people efficient and productive and enabling them to enjoy doing their work because they do it well. Most staff training can be done at the place of work.

Induction training

Induction training should cover all a new employee needs to know fairly quickly, although not necessarily all on the first day. It should include:

- Whereabouts of facilities (toilet, kettle, etc.)
- Security of personal possessions
- Break times and what people normally do
- Fire precautions and procedures
- Introduction to colleagues

- Whereabouts of materials, equipment etc. needed for the job
- Basic job procedures
- Basic company rules, regulations and customs
- Someone to turn to

It is time-consuming to train new people, but it is better than leaving them to dive in at the deep end. Make a checklist that you and the new employee can work from.

Further training
It is usually not enough to show learners once how to do something, and then expect them to do it to full experienced worker standard (EWS). Try to train people in what to do a little bit at a time, and to follow this sequence:

Explain   *tell* the learner not only what is to be done, but why and how it fits in to other jobs
Demonstrate *show* the learner how to do the job – slowly
Try out   *let* the learner do the job while you are still there to watch
Correct   *put right* any mistakes early on – bad habits are difficult to correct later. This is particularly important where safety is concerned

People need training and re-training all their working lives as laws, systems, machinery and equipment change. Allow your staff the time and the facilities to keep up-to-date.

CHAPTER 11 CHECKLIST
1 Recruitment
- Draw up Job Specification (essential and desirable)
- Design advertisement
- Sift incoming applicants
- Interview only a few, with Schedule of Duties
- Write to successful applicant(s)
- After job accepted, write to unsuccessful applicants
  Useful telephone number: Croner Publishers Ltd – 081 942 8966, publishers of Croner's *Reference Book for Employers*.

2 Pay and conditions
- You must pay
  - agreed pay by agreed method at correct time;
    SSP, if applicable;
    maternity pay, if applicable.
- You must deduct – NI and Income Tax
- You must provide employees with
  - a breakdown of pay and deductions;
    an annual P60;
    a P45, if applicable;
    a written Contract of Employment;
    Employer Liability Insurance cover.

3 Health and safety (HASAWA)
- You must
  - do your best to ensure healthy and safe working conditions;
    record all accidents;
    display the company's health and safety policy, if you employ 5 people or more;
    have adequate fire precautions and procedures.
- You should
  - ensure someone knows about First Aid;
    keep an adequate First Aid box.

4 Data Protection Act
- You must
  - register as a data user if you keep personal details electronically;
    allow employees to examine and update their own records.

5 Staff training
- Make an Induction Training Checklist;
- Allow time and facilities for further training.

12

Opening a Shop

In this Chapter

Siting

Image

Stocktaking

People

Legal requirements

Money

Security

Advertising

Siting

Right for the market
In deciding where your outlet should be sited, it is useful to ask yourself whether what you are offering is largely something which customers will buy on impulse if they happen to see it, or whether it is something they need, so will seek you out, within reason, wherever you happen to be.

This means you have two broad categories from which to choose – prime sites and secondary sites.

PRIME SITES
A prime site is where you will find the 'big boys', the household names which customers expect to find in any worthwhile shopping venue.

Prime sites are expensive, and a question you need to ask yourself is, 'If I choose a unit in a prime site, will people passing my door on their way to the branches of the national multiples be tempted to stop and consider my wares – and will they do it in sufficient numbers to justify the expense?'.

SECONDARY SITES

Secondary sites are located away from the prime site areas. Naturally the outgoings on a secondary site are lower than those for a prime site. The level of trade could well be lower, too, so you will probably need to tell the public that you are there, which means that advertising costs for a secondary site could be greater than those for a prime site.

POSITION

Whether prime or secondary, it is worth considering the position of your outlet. For example, would you want to be actually fronting onto the street with pedestrians and traffic passing by or would you prefer to be within a shopping centre?

In considering a site it might be worth seeing who your neighbours will be. What type of goods will they be offering? Will they be indirect competition with you? Will they attract people who might equally be interested in what you have to offer?

Size and shape

Two units with the same square footage could offer good or bad possibilities depending on the shape and the type of stock to be fitted into it. So before tramping off to the agents or around the town centres, consider:

- the optimum size of the unit you need (do not forget stockroom and office space as well)
- the most appropriate shape for the type of business you are intending to run

For example, a deep, narrow shop with very little frontage would be acceptable for a counter service operation – like a jeweller's or a motor accessories shop – but would be unsuitable for a self-service shop – like a mini-market – where customers need more space to walk around selecting their own items.

Decide how far either side of the 'ideal' you are prepared to go, and try to stick to it.

Rent and rates
The shape as well as the size of your unit will have an effect on the expenses. This is because of the way the rental is calculated. The floor area of the shop is divided into zones, with each zone attracting a different level of rent; the zone nearest the front of the shop being the most expensive, so that the rent for a deep, narrow-fronted shop is less than for a shallow, wide-fronted one.

Public transport and parking
Customers need to be able to get to and from your shop easily and conveniently, whether by public transport or under their own steam. When deciding on the siting of your potential outlet, ease of access for customers is something else to consider.

Access for deliveries
As well as thinking about how convenient it is for your customers to get to your store, it is as well to take into account how your stock will be delivered to you in the first place.

For any potential site, see what access there is for suppliers' or carriers' vehicles, and how easy it is to transfer items from a vehicle to your goods in area.

The competition
Consider whether it would be to your advantage to open up a shop opposite an existing outlet which sells a similar range of goods to you:

Advantages	customers can easily make comparisons between different outlets offering similar goods; you can highlight your business with special offers or other features which the competition is not doing
Disadvantages	customers continue to support the existing outlet through force of habit; competitors can anticipate your opening, and mount their own campaigns to distract attention from you in those critical early days.

130

You might then think it wise to set up amongst outlets which offer goods different from those you are planning to sell, so that you are, in effect, the sole supplier in that particular locality.

Image

The general image or impression that a retail outlet presents to the public at large depends on a number of factors, any of which, if not up to standard or of the wrong sort, can damage the overall effect. Even opening hours can contribute to the image of a business by giving an idea of the degree of service available.

Personal service or self service

Once upon a time pretty well everything was sold across the counter, it was the accepted way of doing things. Those days are long gone, although the craze for throwing out counters and going over entirely to self service has now diminished, and it is more usual to find a mixture of these methods.

Whenever self service is used in an outlet, whether wholly or in part, it is always necessary to have somebody available at the cash point to handle customers' purchases. This person can be involved in other duties, but must always be alert to the needs of customers at the cash point, because the essence of the self service system is convenience, and your image could be damaged if customers were kept waiting unnecessarily at the cash point for someone to take the money for their goods.

Fixtures and fittings

The way your stock is presented to customers will depend a great deal on the type of fixture you are using. If you are taking over a unit you might well feel that you can make do with the fixtures left by the previous occupier. If yours is quite a different type of business, though, it might not be a wise decision if it means your stock is not shown off to the best advantage. Perhaps a slight adaptation will do the trick, but it could be a false economy if you are not doing justice to your stock.

A basic requirement of any fixture is that it is appropriate to the type of stock it is meant to hold. It needs to be secure, functional and easy to restock. Some fixtures are made to store back-up stock in drawers or cupboards which makes re-stocking easy and convenient.

Decor and lighting

Outward appearances are important to a retail outlet. Look at the various styles of decoration used by businesses, as well as the variety of colour schemes and try to decide what would be the most suitable decoration for the outside of your premises.

Having made the premises look attractive and inviting from the outside, you must continue that appeal into the interior. Do your research again, and see what other people do, particularly in your line of business.

A very important aspect of your internal decorations is the lighting. This really is an area which needs to be considered carefully: consider level of lighting, type of lighting (fluorescent, spot, and so on), direction of lighting and use of natural light.

Range of stock

Stock is money, and stock on the shelves is money waiting to be transferred to the cash register drawer. You must invest money in stock or you will not have anything to sell, though of course it is not simply a case of getting hold of some stock lines and hoping for the best.

Whatever type of retail business you intend to run it is necessary to have a carefully-considered range of stock, sufficient to offer customers a suitable choice. Getting the balance right is the key; there must not be so much as to be confusing, nor yet too little for the choice to be unreasonably restricted.

So, do you try and go for the image of:

    having whatever customers are likely to want,

or satisfying the majority, leaving the minority customers to seek satisfaction elsewhere,

or specialising, and catering for the minority?

The contribution which stock makes to the image of your business should not be underestimated. Being the prime means of generating your profit, it makes sense to use it to create a favourable image for your business.

Suppliers

What have suppliers to do with image? A simple answer to that question must be, a lot. It is your suppliers on whom you rely to see that you receive that all-important stock we have just been thinking about.

What you are looking for in a supplier is a reliable service, a continuity of supply and an acceptable range of lines. Unless you can get these your image is going to suffer with your customers if they keep finding you are out of stock of the lines they want to buy, particularly the popular ones.

Opening hours

The trend today is for more and more retail outlets to be open for six day trading. This arrangement might not be quite so easy for you if you are working on your own. It might mean that you close for half a day according to local custom, or as dictated by local bye-laws. If your unit is situated within a shopping centre, your opening hours will be dictated by the rules of the establishment.

Whatever the situation, you must make sure that your opening hours enhance your image rather than detract from it. Your image must be that you are there and open for business when customers want to spend their money.

Stocktaking

Stocktaking is an exercise to establish a current record of stock in hand at any given time. This is necessary, not only to establish the number of items, but also the cash value.

Stocktaking is a task undertaken at least once a year for the inclusion of the stock value in the annual accounts. In practice a full stocktaking could well be done twice yearly or even quarterly. It is possible that in certain sections within a shop stock would need to be taken weekly, or, in the case of very perishable items, daily, to provide the basis for an effective stock and order system.

We are concerned here, though, with the general stocktake. Accuracy is paramount for a stocktaking exercise. It is not a job to be rushed or fitted in between other things; it needs full concentration to get it right. This is why, very likely, you will find yourself doing this job out of trading hours, or at a weekend when the shop is closed.

The overall rule to follow for a successful stocktake is for everything to be methodical – the preparation, the execution, the follow-up.

Preparation
Have the sheets you intend to use for the stocktaking clearly identified – at least numbered in sequence. Make sure *all.* are accounted for both before and after the stocktake.

Execution
The method you use to record your stock will depend on the type of business you have. In some cases you will write out a description of the item together with the selling price (retail stock is generally recorded at selling price), or it might be more suitable simply to head the record sheets with prices, and fill in the numbers of the items under the appropriate headings.

It is vital to mark in some way the areas which have been counted to avoid sections being missed or counted twice – a simple chalk mark on the floor or fixture might be sufficient.

Follow-up
When the counting has been completed, make sure all the stock-taking sheets have been collected in and are accounted for.

The graft of counting all the figures and arriving at a grand total for the value of the stock has now to be done.

People

People form an important part of a retail outlet. How many people you will need in your shop will relate to your pattern of trading. You will need to consider whether to use all full-time staff, or perhaps supplement these with part-timers for peak trading times.

Will your staff be male or female, or male *and* female, and which jobs will be most suited to each?

You will need to decide how your staff will be dressed; whether they will be provided with a uniform, or whether ordinary everyday clothes will be suitable – is suitable formal or casual? What will *you* be wearing?

The hours of work will relate both to trade and financial considerations. Remember there is more to paying staff than just wages, for instance, you are responsible for NI contributions.

You will need to devise suitable conditions of employment for potential members of staff. These will include the type of facilities you will need – or would be prepared – to provide, such as toilet and washing facilities, a cloakroom locker, providing suitable security for personal belongings, and dining facilities, even if it is simply tea and coffee making facilities.

Legal requirements

Many of the legal aspects of employing staff are dealt with in Chapter 11. In addition, when running a shop you should know the provisions of:

> The Trades Description Act
> Sale of Goods Act
> Offices, Shops and Railway Premises Act
> Consumer Protection legislation
> Local bye-laws
> Fire prevention requirements

All the legislation is drafted to make sure shopkeepers sell goods which are of 'merchantable quality', properly described and at a price which is fair to the shopkeeper and the consumer.

If you do not know the necessary details of the law relating to keeping a shop, contact the Trading Standards Officer for your local authority.

The Fire Brigade will advise you on what you must do to qualify for a Fire Certificate for your premises.

You will need to have third party insurance for your staff and customers – consult an insurance broker who specialises in small shops.

Money

A retail shop, by its very nature, is bound to be involved in money. You will need to consider how best to handle cash, cheques and credit cards at the point of sale. This will require a set procedure to be devised, and it is important that everybody involved keeps to the system. For this to happen it would probably be helpful to have your procedure written down.

The taking of money at the cashpoint can be a good opportunity to record those details which can provide useful management information, for example, by dissecting sales into suitable groups either by product, department or section. This will be a simple and effective way of creating data for management control, such as the basis for a stock and order system.

At certain times moneys will need to be banked. Establish a regular routine for this, but preferably not a regular route to and from the bank premises. We will consider this further in the next section – Security.

The two essential elements for this task are the preparation of moneys for banking, and the recording of banking transactions. The underlying requirement for this is accuracy. For this to be achieved, once again a definite procedure or system must be established and conscientiously followed by all concerned.

Security

Security should be a continual theme in all aspects of business activity. In this section we will consider four important areas: staff, stock, money and premises.

Staff

It is useful to instil into all members of staff that they should be security-minded, in relation to the stock and moneys of the business as well as their own personal belongings. Try to make them realise that it is as much in their own interest as it is for the business always to be alert to situations where security is not all it might be. Encourage staff to come to you about any apparent lapses in security procedures, and with ideas for improving security arrangements – be sure to be receptive when they do. Security is an important subject which concerns every members of staff in some way or another – it helps if they are aware of this.

Stock

The security of stock should be a continuous and conscious process. In the sales area, apart from stock actually on display, remember security includes accurate ringing up of prices, and being aware of the various dodges which can be used by customers for taking stock items past a cashpoint without paying for them. For example, taking items through in their own bags, hiding items in pockets or under coats, switching low-priced tickets onto high-priced items, not completely clearing a wire basket or trolley, are all methods used by customers to avoid payment.

In the storage area the accurate checking in of deliveries of stock is a very important part of stock security: a business cannot afford to pay suppliers for items of stock it never actually received.

If your shop is likely to handle highly pilferable items – perhaps lines which are small in size but high in value – then consider the best arrangements you can make for their security, for example, a locked security case in the storage area, and keeping them behind glass or behind the counter in the sales area. Perhaps alarmed wires threaded through stock items in the sales area, as often seen on displays of radios etc., could be effective.

Money

Security and money would seem naturally to go together. Once again, there are various situations to consider, and to decide on set procedures or systems to meet them.

The simple device of making sure the cash register drawer is kept open for the least possible time, and certainly firmly shut between the end of one customer's order and starting the next, is a good security system to adopt.

Where cash is stored, security should be as effective as possible. Even if you cannot run to a separate 'custom-built' cash office, try to ensure that the area is as secure as possible during the time that cash is actually being handled and stored.

Whatever the situation, some form of safe would be required; take advice on this from your local crime prevention officer. Incidentally, one has to remember floor loadings when considering the installation of a safe, the floor has to be strong enough to hold it; safe companies will no doubt be pleased to advise you.

We mentioned earlier that we would consider the security aspects of banking. Decide *how* you are intending to transport moneys to and from your bank. The varying of times and route as far as is reasonable is a simple, but effective method. If it is also possible to vary the personnel involved occasionally, that could be useful.

There are several security firms who will undertake to carry moneys to and from the bank on your behalf. Talk to other businesses and to your bank manager, and try to get as much independent advice as possible about the various security firms who operate in your area before committing yourself; once again a talk with your local crime prevention officer might prove fruitful.

Premises

There is a great variety of devices designed to offer security for premises, ranging from the simple idea of placing convex mirrors at strategic points within the sales or storage areas to allow vision of otherwise blind spots, to complicated networks of video cameras and monitors. The aim is to use a system which is the most appropriate to your needs and the needs of your premises.

Do not overlook the traditional alarm bell, particularly one which can be connected to your local police station. Suitable padlocks can provide adequate security for everyday situations inside and outside the building. Keeping doors open for the least possible time, particularly at Goods In when receiving deliveries is a sensible security measure.

You can still find shops which have the old fashioned hanging bell on a spring over the shop door; at least a variation on that theme lets you know that somebody has entered the premises if you have been called away from the sales area.

Ask advice of your local crime prevention officer as well as your insurance company on the subject of security of premises. It could save you spending too much money – and losing a great deal of money and stock.

Advertising

Potential customers will need to know that you and your shop are there, so you need to be alert to all possibilities for advertising your business. This need not restrict itself solely to advertising material.

138

Methods

For example, if you will be needing staff for your shop, remember that you, yourself, will be advertising your business by your appearance, manner and so forth during interviews with applicants: an excellent opportunity for creating a good business image.

Produce some suitable material – well presented – for applicants to take home: another good and subtle way of getting your name known in these critical early stages. For example, give candidates a small leaflet setting out the basic hours and working conditions, holidays and so on. Make sure the shop's name and logo are prominently displayed on the leaflet. You should also take the trouble to notify unsuccessful applicants – it is worth the price of a few stamps in goodwill.

For your more formal advertising, you will no doubt make use of the local press. Compile a Press Release feature about you and your business and talk to the advertising manager of the paper about a combined campaign – involving some straight advertising (which you pay for) and an advertising feature (which you get for free) on your business.

A less formal means of advertising, but one which could be effective for advertising the location of your premises, is a door-to-door leaflet distribution within your catchment area. Some local papers will undertake this task for you – it could be worth raising the matter when talking about advertising matters generally. Have a look at Chapter 5 to remind yourself of things to think about when producing an advertising leaflet.

Do not overlook the opportunity which the shop premises themselves provide for advertising. The actual shop front will present an image to the passing public. Suitable posters on the windows will carry particular messages, even if it is only to advertise the day of opening of your new enterprise.

Timing

Having considered *what* advertising methods to use, you should also think about *when* to use them. Timing is significant, particularly when advertising something new, like the opening of a new shop.

Your 'Coming shortly' or 'Opening soon' advertising which could be appearing in the local press, should be timed to arouse initial interest (the AIDA formula, see Chapter 5, page 41), followed by a second wave of advertising to carry on the momentum up to the moment of opening with, perhaps, a final reminder to say 'We are now here'.

As well as the general press advertising, you might consider a leaflet distribution related specifically to the day of opening, combined with a special offer valid only for opening day.

Opening day
When the great day arrives, make sure you try to get the most out of it. The use of large posters on the shop windows announcing the fact is probably a good start.

Are you considering having someone special to declare the premises open? If so, will the public come to see that person rather than buy things from your shop? Remember the value of the Press Release and of press coverage; make sure a photographer is ready to hand.

Maybe a special offer – a voucher for a free item or a reduction of a set amount handed to the first 50 customers to enter the shop – could provide useful advertising and goodwill (except from customer No. 51!).

Do not overlook the value of giving a personal welcome to those first customers as they enter the door. Putting the human touch to a business enterprise, if done well and sincerely, can only be of value to that business.

CHAPTER 12 CHECKLIST
1 Siting
   Consider:
   - Prime site or secondary
   - Street or precinct
   - Size and shape
   - Rent and rates implications
   - Public transport and parking
   - Access for deliveries
   - The competition

2 Image
   Consider:
   - Personal service or self service

- Fixtures and fittings
- Decor and lighting
- Range of stock
- Suppliers
- Opening hours

3 Stocktaking
- When will you do this?
- What preparations have you made?
- What are your plans for counting the stock?

4 People
- How many – full or part time?
- What hours of work?
- What conditions of employment?

5 Legal requirements
- Do you know the law relating to your type of business? If not, consult the Local Authority's Trading Standards officer
- Are your premises worthy of a Fire Certificate? Consult the Fire Brigade.
- Have you got third party insurance? Consult your insurance broker or insurance company.

6 Money
- What is your system for accepting cash, cheques, credit cards, etc.?
- Is it written down?
- Does everyone know it?
- What is your system for recording and banking your takings?

7 Security
- What do your staff know about security?
- How secure is your stock
  (a) in the sales area
  (b) in the stockroom
  (c) at goods in?
- What are your security arrangements for money in the shop and money in transit to the bank?

- Are your premises fully secure at all times of the day and night?

8 Advertising
Consider:
- Press
- Leaflet drops
- Posters
- Opening day

NOTE More detailed information and guidance about opening a shop and the retailing industry in general can be found in *People in Retailing* and *Profitable Retailing* also by Vera Hughes and David Weller (published by Macmillan).

13

Import and Export

In this Chapter

Import   *Ordering from abroad; Documentation; Clearing goods through customs, and transportation; Methods of payment; Insurance*

Export: *Should you export?; Where to get help*

Import and export are often lumped together, as they are in the heading to this chapter, but, apart from the documentation, they are quite different. A very small firm (a sole trader) might want to import items (gifts, for example). Export is for those who have solid experience of marketing and selling their product or service on the home market before they embark on exporting. It could be part of expanding your business, but should not be undertaken from the start.

This chapter can only give you very broad guidelines for importing and exporting. For details of what you should do see *Importing for the Small Business* by Mag Morris published by Kogan Page Second Edition 1988 and *Export for the Small Business* by Henry Deschampsneufs published by Kogan Page Second Edition 1988. These are excellent books for anyone starting out in Import and Export.

Import

To import sounds more daunting than it actually is. You are merely buying from an overseas supplier instead of a home supplier, and the difference is all to do with procedures, currency and time – things which can be calculated or learnt. We deal here with the mechanics of getting the goods from overseas to your place of work – not with choosing suppliers and negotiating deals.

Ordering

Before you place an order you should get a firm quotation from your supplier. Be very specific about what you want on the quotation; this is best done by a formal request for a quotation setting out:

- Who you are and what your business is
- Who your bankers are, to help establish your creditworthiness
- The goods or services you want, and how they are to be packed and marked
- Possible questions
- Delivery dates and terms
- What insurance arrangements you intend to use

Once you have a firm quotation, you can place your order.

When you place an order in the UK, you know that you must be precise in what you are ordering and where it should be delivered. You also have to take into account delivery times, carriage charges and discounts.

Ordering from abroad is no different. You can order by phone or fax, but the order should be confirmed in writing on your headed paper. Remember to agree with your supplier:

- Quantity, description and price
- Method of despatch (air, sea or land)
- Method of delivery (post, courier, etc.) and delivery destination (port, warehouse, etc.)
- Delivery times, which are likely to be longer, but not necessarily
- The point at which the insurance by the supplier stops and the insurance by you begins (see Insurance page 146, later in this chapter)
- Whether the prices quoted include insurance
- Carriage charges

144

- Discounts
- Method of payment

As you can see, the 'extras' are all to deal with the goods coming over a longer distance.

Documentation

Advice Note	On receipt of your order, the supplier should confirm to you all the details mentioned above, including date of expected despatch and length of delivery time
Bill of Lading	This is the receipt given by a ship's master to the supplier of goods, stating in detail the goods loaded on board the ship. The Bill of Lading is an important part of the papers which travel with goods being imported or exported
Air Waybill	This is a sort of aviation Bill of Lading. It is a contract of carriage when goods are sent by air, and acts as a receipt for the goods. It is made out by the airline
Pro Forma Invoice	You will also receive a Pro Forma Invoice, probably stating the preferred method of payment

These are the most common items of documentation. For details of customs and other documents, seek advice from your clearing agent, or from the Mag Morris book.

Customs and transportation

If you are intending to import fairly large quantities of goods, it could be wise, to start with, to use a clearing agent, who will deal with all the customs and transport side of it for you. Seek advice from your local Chamber of Commerce.

If you are importing on a very small or limited basis, the Post Office is an excellent transporter of goods. Your supplier will complete all the customs documentation necessary. If the order is a sample, and not for onward sale by you, ask the supplier to mark the goods 'Sample only – of no commercial value'. This should mean that you do not have to pay customs duty.

The postman can collect duty and VAT up to £50.00; otherwise you will have to collect your packages from the sorting office, and pay any VAT and duty due at that point. You will probably have to pay a Post Office clearance fee. Keep the Post Office label on the package, as this will constitute your VAT receipt for book-keeping purposes.

Methods of payment
The main methods of payment are:

CASH
Sent by registered post. This is popular for small orders among third world countries

VIA THE BANK

Banker's Order	You need to order the Order from the bank, allow 24 hours, collect it yourself and post it. The bank charges a fee. A Banker's Order is negotiable (in other words, it is like cash) so should be securely handled
Telegraphic or Airmail Transfer	Called SWIFT. You have to go to the bank to sign the form. The money is transferred immediately to the supplier's bank account. You need to know the supplier's bank and name and number of the account. You pay a fee at this end, and the recipient pays a fee at the other end. The payment can be sent 'priority' for which an extra fee is charged
Letter of Credit	This method of payment is generally used for large amounts (£1000 and over). You open a Letter of Credit through your own bank, setting out the terms and conditions under which you intend to pay. The Letter of Credit is generally made 'Irrevocable' which means that the terms and conditions cannot be altered without agreement

146

between you and your supplier – that is, you cannot 'stop' the payment. There are various other safeguards for you and for your supplier; from your point of view a Letter of Credit normally means that no money will be transferred until the supplier has despatched the goods and prepared all the necessary documentation. (Some suppliers ask for payment in advance, in which case a different method of payment must be used.)

Bill of Exchange
This works the other way round. Your supplier draws a draft on you via his bank with the necessary documentation, once he has despatched the goods. Your bank presents you with the draft and the documents, so that you can collect the goods once you have paid or accepted the draft (which at that point becomes a bill). This normally means that you do not have to pay for the goods until you have received them. Suppliers are not usually keen to extend this credit unless they know you well and are assured of your creditworthiness

VIA THE POST OFFICE
An International Payment Coupon (rather like a Postal Order) can be bought at the Post Office and sent by post to the supplier. It is suitable for small amounts.

Insurance
You need to be sure that your goods are insured until they reach your doorstep. These are the most common terms used when despatching goods:

FOB (Free on Board)
The price quoted includes everything until the goods are loaded onto the

	ship or plane. This does not include insurance
CIF (Cost Insurance Freight)	Means that everything is covered, including insurance, up to delivery at your warehouse *except* the cost of transport from the port or airport in the UK. You will have to arrange and pay for the cost of this transport, but the goods remain insured
C&F (Cost and Freight)	Means that the goods are *not* insured so you will have to make your own insurance arrangements

As you can see, it is important that you are clear about the terms under which your goods will be supplied, so make sure they appear on the quotation you have requested.

Importing small quantities of goods is quite easy, particulary if you use the postal services. Importing large quantities is obviously more complicated. Seek all the advice you can before you start. Importing from EEC countries from 1992 should be a simpler matter – it remains to be seen whether it really is.

Export

There are many rewards to be gained from a sound export business, but you should not embark on this until you are sure you have a viable and solid business base in the UK.

When exporting, you will need to consider all the aspects of selling that you have been carrying on, but at a distance and in a market which you probably do not know. Think of carrying out market research, marketing, selling, transporting, getting paid and all the other aspects of your business in another country, and you will see that exporting is not for the beginner. Having said that, your product or service might be a very marketable commodity abroad.

You will need help to set about exporting your product, so this chapter will confine itself to giving you guidance on where to look for that help.

British Overseas Trade Board (BOTB)	The Board is there to help UK firms make a success of their

exporting business. Your point of contact is your BOTB regional office.

The Board publishes some very useful leaflets, giving guidance on the things you should consider and when you should start. The leaflets include: *Now's the Time to Export – First Steps for Smaller Firms* and *Exporting for the Smaller Firm.* They are obtainable from your BOTB regional office (see The phone Book) or from BOTB Marketing and Briefing Unit, 1 Victoria Street, London SW1H 0ET

The Simplification of International Trade Procedures Board (SITPRO)

This organisation tries to simplify procedures and paperwork and generally help the efficiency of export and payment. They publish an Export Documentation Starter Kit. The contact is Almack House, 26–28 King Street, London SW1Y 3QW (Telephone: 071 930 0532)

Banks, Chambers of Commerce, Export Houses

Details of the type of help these can give are in the BOTB 'Now's the Time to Export' publication.

Export for the Small Business

This book, by Henry Deschamps-neufs, mentioned at the start of this chapter, goes into considerable detail on:
- decisions you should take;
- market research;
- product modifications and marketing;
- pricing;
- potential customers;
- selling;

- transport;
- payment, etc.

and finishes with a list of useful addresses and contacts.

Other publications are recommended in the BOTB leaflet

CHAPTER **13** CHECKLIST

1 Import (Use this checklist for each order you place)
   - Have you got a firm quotation?
   - Does the Quotation cover all details?
   - Has all documentation been completed?
   - How will you handle customs?
   - How will you get the goods to your doorstep?
   - Which method of payment will you use?
   - Are your goods properly insured?

2 Export
   - Are you ready to export yet?

If the answer is 'Yes', seek help and advice from BOTB, SITPRO and various publications. Do not try to go it alone.

14

Specially for Women

In this Chapter

Running a home and a
    business
Children and other
    dependants
Your health

Your business image
Money
Women's organisations and
    training

This chapter has been written specially for women and is written from a woman's point of view because women often have problems and calls on their time and energies which men do not have. This is particularly true for women who run a home as well as a business – it is often the woman who actually organises the running of the home, even when the domestic chores and care of the children are shared equally. Much of what is said here applies to a man who has to run a home and look after children as well as run his business, but these men are still in the minority.

The chapter is not only for women who have a husband or partner at home and children: much of it is for any woman who is starting to run her own business, whatever her domestic circumstances.

Running a home and a business

Starting your own business is hard work, and takes a lot of time and energy. Unless the domestic side of your life is well organised, you will find it very difficult to give the business the concentration it needs. If you get to work worrying about the ironing which did not get done, you will find it difficult to give your whole attention to your business matters. You need to be either the sort of person who does not mind living in chaos at home – and whose family does not mind living in chaos either – or the sort of person who is well organised.

Every woman has her own way of organising her domestic life, so this section does not say that you should or should not do certain things. It tries to give you some ideas which will help you to organise yourself and your family to include the extra business dimension.

Planning ahead

No matter how much other people in the household help, it is normally left to the woman to plan the routine, which includes either shopping or, at the very least, making a shopping list.

If you have been used to shopping frequently – perhaps a little every day or so – you will need to think about shopping less often, so that it is not so time-consuming. If you run your freezer efficiently, you do not need to shop more often than once a week, provided you plan ahead. Some women do a 'bake-in' for the whole week ahead as well.

It is useful to keep a note in your diary of what everyone else is doing, as well as your own business engagements, and a family diary or wall chart is a great help. If you can persuade members of the household to declare what they are going to be doing at least a week ahead, and put it down in the family diary, it helps you to plan who needs to eat what, and when. Try not to keep too many diaries (one personal and one family should be enough) or you will find it difficult to keep them up-to-date.

You will also need to plan ahead for such things as:

- Children's activities
- Business dinners
- Family holidays and breaks
- Visits to the vet (if you have pets)
- Visits from service engineers, the piano tuner, etc.
- Clothes shopping
- Social and leisure activities

It might sound a bit regimented if you are not used to planning your life in this way, but if you like to live an organised sort of life, you will find that careful planning is essential to your peace of mind and the success of your business. It also gives the family a sense of security, although you have to guard against a lack of flexibility: always having smoked mackerel salad on a Friday starts as a joke, but can finally become an irritant.

Division of labour
If you are to run your business successfully, you really do need the support of the people at home, not just occasionally, but all the time. It is illogical for people to sit around waiting for you to get home to get the evening meal: perhaps a 'first in starts the meal' routine would work in your household.

Each family will have its own way of sorting out who does what, but it is important that everyone, including the smallest of the children, does something on a regular basis. Three-year-olds can tidy their toys away; five-year-olds can dust; ten-year-olds can help prepare the vegetables; fourteen-year-olds can cope with washing, ironing, mending and cooking. Everyone can help with the washing up and the cleaning. Discuss these things with the family, and see who can do what, and how they can best fit it in with their own timetable. Obviously only adults can drive cars, but almost everyone can push a hoover around.

In some households the chores seem to fall naturally into male and female jobs; in others, who does what is by preference. Women often find that only they are prepared to clean the lavatory and the bath. You can encourage everyone in the family to look after their personal belongings, which means both male and female cleaning their shoes and doing their mending – again there is no logical reason why they should not.

In a busy household the garden often gets neglected. If you are a tidy person, this will niggle away at the back of your mind, particularly if you care what the neighbours say – and many people do. It is helpful to have a garden which is easy to cope with, and which other family members do not mind working in. Go in for easily-kept lawns and shrubs, or patios. Plenty of ground cover keeps the weeds at bay. No garden will look reasonable if left totally unattended – even if your garden is a window box, the plants still need watering – but you can make it easier for yourself and other members of the household if you plan the garden carefully and agree with the others on who will do what. Gardening can be a very good way of getting away from the business for a while, and you will need to do that from time to time.

Using help
Some women manage to do everything superbly well: they run a business, a house and a social life, and have really good relationships with people at home and at work, and you wonder how they do it.

One of the secrets often is that they use all the help they can get, both human and mechanical. Reliable help with the cleaning, washing, ironing and mending is not easy to find, but if you can find someone at least to do the heavy cleaning, it is well worth the expense. You need not feel guilty or inadequate because you are paying someone else to do what perhaps you consider is your responsibility. You are earning money elsewhere, and you cannot do everything yourself; employing someone to help in the home or the garden benefits you and the person you are employing to do the job. It may take time to find the right person, but it is worth persevering. Using help is a strength, not a weakness.

You should also use all the mechanical help you can get, such as a really efficient washing machine and dryer, a dishwasher, a microwave, if you like that method of cooking. Use appliances which make your life, and that of everyone else in the household, easier. This might mean updating your appliances more frequently than you are used to doing. It is normally worth the money and the effort.

Time and people
Your business will find it more difficult to thrive if your domestic background is unstable. This means making time to be with your home partner and the children, if you have any. You might have to work some evenings and weekends, but if you make it every evening and weekend, undercurrents of dissatisfaction are likely to start up at home, and you will lose the goodwill and support of the people you need most.

Children need a stable home base, and they need to know that their parents have the time and the interest to care about their activities and their worries. This is common sense, of course, but it is amazing how easy it is for a woman to get caught up in the excitement and freedom of doing her own thing, and to forget, very gradually, how much she is needed and wanted at home. It is a fine balance to strike, but if sensitively handled need not mean that either home or business has to suffer.

Children and other dependents

You might be the type of woman who feels guilty at letting other people look after her children or other dependents – an elderly relative, perhaps. Very few women escape this sense of guilt at some time or other, particularly when they leave a new baby in the care of others for the first time. Other members of the family, perhaps your own parents, can often make you feel guilty as well, sometimes quite deliberately.

One way of coping with this is to acknowledge the sense of guilt, and then do everything that you can to make sure that your children and other dependents are well cared for when you are not with them. This section will concentrate on caring for children.

Nannies

Nannies look after children in your own home. This can be as a live-in nanny, a daily nanny, or one who lives in during the week and goes home at weekends.

Some nannies have been to top-class training establishments, and are fully qualified in all aspects of child care. The training is thorough, and expensive. A qualified nanny will be seeking a well-paid position, often as a live-in nanny, with excellent domestic facilities, working conditions and hours. These are often the nannies who answer advertisements in *The Lady*, which seems to be the leading 'top nanny' recruitment medium, if one can put it that way. These nannies will have excellent references, and can be relied upon to do a thoroughly competent and reliable job, combined with real care for the children, in a suitable household.

If you are looking for a less highly-qualified nanny, who perhaps will look after your children on a daily basis, and sometimes on a job-share basis (some hours or days with you, some with another family), look in local nanny agencies, Job Centres and advertisements in the local paper. You can advertise in the local paper yourself, of course.

Agencies do not necessarily 'screen' the applicants for your particular job – some do and some do not. You usually have to pay a registration fee, as an employer, and the agency will send you prospective nannies for you to interview. You need to find out from the agency what you are paying for – it might be just the introduction, or the agency might do a certain amount of selection on your behalf. They will need to know how much you are prepared to pay (usually by the hour); an agency or a Job Centre can advise you on this.

What are you looking for in a nanny? Obviously someone who likes and can deal with children and has a fondness for them. When you interview a prospective nanny, make sure it is at a time when your children are around and awake. Let the nanny play with them or hold them, and watch the reactions of the nanny and the children.

It is also important that the nanny's personality is compatible with yours. If you have a fairly strong personality (and you have to be able to acknowledge this), a nanny with an equally forceful outlook on life could cause problems. On the other hand, you do not want anyone who is not capable of following instructions and taking decisions when necessary. There can be clashes of culture as well as personality; young women sometimes move from one part of the country to another, or from one country to another, and their diet and background could be quite different from yours and what you want for your children. This need not be a problem if you are clear about what you want, and if you are both prepared to be understanding and a little flexible. It is something to consider when engaging a nanny to look after your children.

A nanny will expect to do everything connected with the children, according to the hours of work agreed. At the start you will need to make lists of the children's routines, roughly what you would like them to eat for their meals, what you want them to wear, and so on. A nanny will not expect to do housework, except where it is directly connected with the children – their clothes, their meals. Unless you have fairly well-delineated areas of work, there can be conflict between a nanny and, say, the person who does the cleaning in the house: the one could resent what the other does and does not do. Incidentally, cleaning ladies often get paid rather more than nannies.

Mother's help

A Mother's Help is someone (usually a woman) who is prepared to do a bit of everything – looking after the children and some domestic work. These women are not often professionally qualified, but are quite capable of looking after children and doing some of the domestic chores, such as light cleaning, washing and ironing. They would expect to be paid more then just a nanny or just a cleaner, but could be less expensive than employing both.

You will find Mother's Helps through agencies, Job Centres and advertisements in the local press. You both (employer and employed) need to be clear about what you expect, what the job entails and what the payment is to be. A Mother's Help is also someone who is going to look after *your* children, so you need to be just as careful about selection as if you were employing a nanny.

Au pairs

These are (usually) young women from abroad whose main aim is to live in England for a while to improve their English. They will normally want to live in with the family, so need reasonable living accommodation and time off. They will probably be happy to do light housework as well as look after the children.

Because an au pair is usually a young person, you will have a certain amount of responsibility for her welfare in this country, and you will probably be required to allow her specific time off to pursue her English studies.

It is helpful to employ au pairs through agencies who specialise in this area of work, because they can advise you on your responsibilities as well as what you can expect from an au pair. An au pair will not expect to be paid a great deal of money, but she will expect to live and be treated as part of the family.

Childminders

If your business allows you to work regular hours and you can be sure to deliver and collect your children, a registered childminder can be a good way of making sure your children are well cared for. Childminders are often women who have children of their own at home, and are happy to add to their family on a regular basis and look after other people's children as well as their own.

Childminders do not have to be registered, but it is perhaps safer to go to a childminder who is registered with the local authority, because their facilities, safety and competence are monitored. Lists of registered childminders can be obtained from the Social Services via the DSS. Many childminders are prepared to look after your children for long hours, or for odd hours, provided it is on a regular basis.

Illness and holidays

It is when your children are ill that you are likely to feel most torn between your business and your family. Perhaps you have an important client to meet, and a phone call comes through that your child is ill. What do you do? Perhaps your instincts are to rush home and let the client know that the meeting will have to be postponed. On the other hand, you are in business, and if you have not got a business partner who can cover for you, perhaps your domestic partner, or another member of the family, can cope with the immediate problem, and you can take it from there. Make all necessary arrangements, and try to put the illness out of your mind until you have completed your business, unless of course it is very serious. Then you can drop everything else and give your child all your attention.

Holidays are another matter and can be planned for. Some local authorities provide facilities for looking after children too young to be left on their own during the school holidays and half terms. One of the benefits of being self-employed is that you can sometimes arrange your workload round school holidays, depending on the nature of the business and the people with whom you work.

If you have to leave young teenagers on their own during the day, they sometimes find it acceptable for you to leave, every morning, a plan of action for the day, which can include jobs to do and, perhaps, outings or activities that you have pre-arranged or for which you have bought a ticket. It takes quite a lot of thought and organisation on your part, but can be useful for only children, or children whose friends have all decided to be away at the same time.

Holidays do not just take care of themselves. Again it helps to plan fairly carefully, but to allow some flexibility.

Other dependents

It depends whether other people who are dependent on you are living in your house or on their own. In either case, if they have been used to having you around, it is going to be difficult for both parties to accept that some of your time is going to be allocated elsewhere. You may face accusations that you are unfeeling, or a hard business-woman, which, again, will make you feel guilty.

As with children, provided you have made every provision possible for the care and welfare of dependent relatives (home helps, local shopping services, meals on wheels), there is no reason why you should not go about your business with a clear mind. Enlist the help of other members of your family, including your own children and your domestic partner, and remember your own brothers and sisters.

Involve dependents in the decisions which have to be made, and share with them as far as possible the excitement – and the worries – of running your own business. It could add an extra dimension to their lives.

Your health

When you are self-employed you cannot afford to be ill, and you usually have not got the time to be ill. Certainly a busy life and being really interested in what you are doing makes you less inclined to have or notice minor ailments.

As far as major illnesses are concerned, you need to do all you can to prevent these. Your lifestyle and regular medical checkups will make sure you are healthy and fit to maintain the energy and stamina which you will certainly need.

Your lifestyle

When you are very busy, you are tempted not to eat properly. Stress and digestive disorders can build up if you never have breakfast, do not stop for lunch, rush home and get the evening meal and then eat it in a hurry. If you can discipline yourself to have a definite break for lunch, even if it is only a short one, your productivity will remain high in the afternoon.

Sometimes you can get caught up in a lot of business lunches; too many of those can ruin your figure as well as your digestion.

However, it is acceptable to be seen not to eat too much at lunchtime and not to drink too much. In fact, women have an advantage here, because they do not have to project a macho image. You can easily drift into high alcohol consumption, but fortunately it is now quite all right to be seen not to drink if you are driving, or to have mineral water with your lunch or dinner wine.

It goes without saying, and is common sense, that a well-balanced diet is what you need to keep healthy. The problem is that you can get so busy trying to run at least two lives at once that you ignore this aspect of your lifestyle, and eat and drink too much or too little.

It is not easy to fit in regular exercise, because often you cannot stick to a very strict timetable. But if you can swim, walk, do keep fit, play tennis or squash or do something in the way of exercise on a regular basis, it will certainly help to keep your body in trim and of course your clothes will look better on you. At the very least, walk up stairs instead of taking lifts, do not ride where you can walk and try to get a little exercise in every day, even if it is only five minutes with the TV first thing in the morning.

Some people seem to survive on very little sleep, and some people need a lot. Whatever your necessary quota, try to make sure that you get it. If someone is ill, you cannot, perhaps, help staying up all night, but it does not do you any good to lie awake worrying – the problem will not be solved, and your body and mind will not be refreshed. Try to finish all you have to do before you go to bed, and be determined to leave everything else until the next day. Some people can catnap during the day, and find this refreshing; if you are that type of person, it can be better to stop off at a motorway service station for fifteen minutes and have a sleep, rather than arrive feeling worn out. If you do decide to sleep in your car, remember to shut all windows and lock all doors for safety's sake, and park in the middle of the car park rather than in a quiet corner.

If you are able to fit it in, it is a good idea to spend some time each week doing something which has nothing to do with work, and nothing to do with home. Regular exercise can be one such activity, but joining a group to share interests or learn something new can be equally relaxing and therapeutic. You need a little time for yourself.

Preventive medicine
If you are self-employed you cannot claim sickness benefit from an

employer or from the state. Some people take out insurance cover for lost earnings if they are sick, as well as covering the cost of treatment to enable them to get back to work as quickly as possible.

Another form of insurance is to have a full, regular medical checkup, probably annually. These are given at Well Woman Clinics, which are sometimes available on the National Health, or privately. A regular checkup means that any illness can be detected at an early stage, and the cure is often swift and complete – less time away from your business. Take advantage of breast screening and cervical smear testing, particularly if you are in the high-risk age groups. There is an Imperial Cancer Research Fund video programme available which shows how valuable the new breast screening programme could be. It is called 'One Woman in Twelve' and is available from Plymouth Medical Films, Palace Vaults, 33 New Street, Barbican, Plymouth PL1 2NA.

As well as detecting the early signs of disease, a doctor giving you regular checkups can also advise you on your general health. It is obvious to you if you are putting on or losing too much weight, but high blood pressure or a high cholesterol level are not obvious. These are checked in a full medical, and your doctor will advise you on diet and exercise.

Addiction to smoking or drugs of any sort, including tranquillisers, will damage your health. If you know you take too many pills, or cannot stop smoking, seek help. You cannot afford to let such things drain away your energies. If you know you suffer from PMT or 'disabling' periods, go to your doctor. There are often things which can be done to alleviate discomfort, and you might as well take the trouble to sort these things out, rather than put up with it every month.

Your health is very precious, and you need to be in good health to run a business successfully. Look after it.

Your business image

You are in business, and need to look, sound and appear businesslike. This means that your whole image should reflect you and the type of business you run. It does not mean that you have to give up your femininity, but nor should you exploit it.

Your appearance

Try to choose a style of dress, makeup and hairstyle which suits you and the image you want to project. This does not necessarily mean that you need to keep up with the latest fashion detail, unless you are in that type of business yourself. It does mean that you need to keep your wardrobe reasonably up-to-date in both style and colour.

It can be a good idea to buy several items which you can mix and match, having chosen your colour scheme for the season or the year. There are many businesses run by women who can advise you on the sort of style and colouring which is the best for you and your particular image. If you are the sort of woman who finds it difficult to decide on what is best for you, a visit to that type of establishment could be a worthwhile investment. You can find their advertisements in professional and business women's magazines and publications.

If your wardrobe and hairstyle have been geared to a home environment, you will need to take time to plan and build up a business wardrobe gradually. Your hair needs to be easy to look after, and yet look smart and stylish, without being way out. A style which can be washed frequently and dried with ease is a great asset – and so is an efficient hairdryer.

Be strict about not driving in business shoes – nothing ruins the heels more quickly. It is worth having a pair of driving shoes which you keep in the car and which you can slip on and off easily. Keep a spare pair of tights or stockings in your briefcase.

Bags and briefcases say a lot about you. If your handbag and briefcase are in a muddle, you will project a muddly image. A slim briefcase, containing only the papers you need for that day, shows an orderly mind, and therefore an orderly way of doing business. If your handbag and briefcase are of good quality they will last longer and project a quality image of you. Buy as good as you can afford. It does not enhance your image to arrive with an overflowing, cheap handbag and a plastic carrier bag!

Your car is part of your appearance, too. It does not matter if it is small and elderly, provided it is well cared for and clean. A car full of children's bits and pieces is not a good idea; try to leave those at home.

Your social skills

Women in business, and particularly women who run their own business, are still women in a man's world. You need to be aware of this and to take account of it in the way you handle situations at meetings, in hotels and socially. Treat men, and women, in a natural, straightforward way, and you will usually find that they respond accordingly. There are things to bear in mind which might help you in these situations.

When greeting anyone for the first time, shake hands, firmly; do the same when saying goodbye. It helps to break down the initial barrier between you and to end a meeting on a friendly note. Most meetings, whether they are large, formal meetings or small, informal ones usually start off with some smalltalk between you and your neighbour. Stick to neutral topics like the weather, the journey or the car park. People do not want to talk, at that stage, about burning issues of the day, or about domestic topics. However, it is useful to keep up-to-date with what is going on in current affairs, the business world and/or sport, so that you can talk with a reasonable amount of knowledge about these things, if the occasion arises.

Accept offers of tea, coffee or other refreshments, and be definite about how you like it. Changing your mind about such apparently trivial matters at the start of a business acquaintance or meeting is not a good beginning.

Some men still regard businesswomen with suspicion. They can feel superior, or threatened, or both. Treat them with quiet confidence, showing that you know your business but have no wish to be over-friendly, and you should not have any problems. Some men are quite happy to do business with women, but still like to treat them *as* women in such matters as opening doors, carrying heavy loads and so on. Do not expect men to do this, but if they wish to do so, accept graciously with a smile and a thankyou. It makes them feel good and will not diminish your standing in any way.

Remember that some decisions are made in the Gents; be aware of several men disappearing at the same time and returning with a united front. If you are aware of such things, you can counteract them if necessary.

Hotels are much better than they used to be about dealing with businesswomen on their own, and some chains, such as Crest, have 'executive women's' rooms. However, some hotels still automatically do such things as making accounts out to 'Mr' and assuming that a man will order and try the wine. It is worthwhile learning about food and wines, if you do not already know these things, so that you can handle situations in bars and restaurants with confidence and ease. You do not have to be over-assertive, but you can make your position known with calm authority, and you should do so.

As a woman starting out in business you need to earn the respect of other business people in all sorts of situations.

Money

Keep your business moneys separate

It is important to keep your business and domestic money separate. From 1990 you will be separately taxed and assessed anyway, as a person rather than as a married woman (if you are married), and this will include your unearned income – building society interest, and so on. But keeping the money separate goes much further than that.

If you start mixing up the money you use for housekeeping with your business money, particularly if part or all of that is supplied by your domestic partner, your book-keeping will get in a hopeless muddle. It is even worth having two purses if you deal in cash – one for the housekeeping, and one for your own personal and business money.

You also have to remember that if you have a business partner, the financial affairs of the business are as much to do with that partner as they are to do with you, and a certain amount of confidentiality should be maintained. Discussing your business finances in detail with your domestic partner can lead to your discussing your business partner's personal finances with your domestic partner. This can be a tricky situation, and needs careful handling, particularly if your domestic partner has always been the one to handle the household finances.

What you can claim for tax purposes

Chapter 8 sets out in some detail what you can and cannot claim for tax purposes.

In addition, women should know that as the tax law stands in 1989/1990, you cannot claim for business clothes, nor for childcare of any sort.

You might be able to claim for domestic cleaning services, if you work from home. Ask your accountant's advice on this, and make sure, before you claim, that your cleaner is declaring that income on his or her tax return.

Pensions

You may or may not be entitled to a full state pension in your own right. If you have only ever paid a married woman's National Insurance stamp or have never paid any National Insurance at all, you will certainly not be entitled to draw your own pension; the cases of this are becoming rarer, because it is only women who are now in their late forties and upwards who were entitled to take this option when they were earning.

In any case you should certainly take out a pension in your own right if you possibly can. For one thing, the payments can be taken into account for tax purposes, and for another, you will ultimately be able to benefit yourself from your own business dealings. It will also give you the continued independence to which you have become accustomed.

Shop around for a pension which is best suited to your needs. Ask your accountant's advice, but be aware that some accountants are tied agents – that is, tied to one insurance company, which might not be the best for you. Try to find an independent accountant or insurance broker.

Your car expenses

If you have been used to driving the family car, a car of your own can be an unexpectedly high expense. It is worth striving to get your own car through the business however, so that you are always independent and mobile.

The business will pay the tax, insurance, purchase and servicing costs, and these will be the same for a woman as for a man, except in one area. If you have been driving the family car and it is insured in your domestic partner's name, you will have to start earning your own no claims bonus from the beginning. The no claims bonus usually belongs to the 'insured', the person the insurance companies reckon does the bulk of the driving. It does not matter if you have done the bulk of the driving, and have never made a claim – you will still have to start from scratch if you now become the insured. This is not a sexist matter, because it would have worked the other way around if you had been the insured; it is just generally more likely that the man was the insured. This can be an additional and unexpected expense.

Women's organisations and training

There are several women's organisations which, as a business woman, you can join for two main purposes: to share ideas, problems and experiences and to learn more about running your own business.

For example 'Women in Enterprise' is a nationwide organisation formed specially for women who run their own businesses. They issue a Newsletter, and have local, regional branches who organise activities to do with women in business.

'Women in Management' and 'Women and Training' (the latter for women who are professional trainers) are much more geared towards women employed by other people. The Professional Women's Association is, as its name implies, for women in the professions, self-employed or not. *Executive Woman* is a useful bi-monthly publication.

As far as training for women in business is concerned, consult your local college. Many run self-assertiveness courses, women into marketing and that type of thing. The Training Agency sponsors courses specially for women: details can be obtained from a Job Centre.

Private training providers, such as The Industrial Society, or The Business Women's Training Institute run courses on a variety of topics, but usually along the lines of confidence building and communication skills. For skill-based topics, such as book-keeping, your local college is probably a better bet.

You need not feel on your own as a woman in business – there are plenty more around.

166

CHAPTER **14** CHECKLIST

Use this list to check your business circumstances as a woman:

1 At home
   - Which aspects of running a home are not well organised?
   - Which chores do I do that other people could do or share?
   - Are there any other labour-saving gadgets I could use?
   - Can I afford someone to do the cleaning/gardening?
   - Do I want someone to help in these areas?

2 Children and other dependents
   Which of these should I look into further?
   - Nannies
   - Mother's Help
   - Childminders
   - Home Helps
   - Meals on Wheels
   - Home Shopping services

3 Health
   - Do I eat the right things?
   - Do I eat at the right times?
   - What regular exercise do I take?
   - Do I have regular medical checkups?
   Useful telephone number: Plymouth Medical Films (breast screening video) – 0752 267711

4 Image
   - What sort of image do I project?
   - What else ought I to do?

5 Money
   - Which aspects do I not understand?
   - Where can I learn about those?
   - Have I got a pension sorted out?

6 Training
   - Is there anything else I need to learn, as a woman?
   - If so, where do I go for help?

Useful addresses:

WOMEN IN ENTERPRISE, St Gabriels House, 24 Laburnum Road, Wakefield WF1 3Q5 (Telephone: 0924 361789)

WOMEN IN MANAGEMENT, 64 Marryat Road, Wimbledon, London SW19 5BN (Telephone: 081 946 1238)

WOMEN AND TRAINING, Hewmar House, 120 London Road, Gloucester GL1 3TL (Telephone: 0452 309330)

THE BUSINESS WOMEN'S TRAINING INSTITUTE, 793 Western Road, Slough, Berks SL1 4HP (Telephone: 0753 820277)

THE INDUSTRIAL SOCIETY, 3 Carlton House Terrace, London SW1 (Telephone: 071 839 4300)

EXECUTIVE WOMAN, Tempus House of Publishers Ltd, 342/362 Corn Exchange Buildings, Manchester M4 3BU

15

Help and Advice

In this Chapter
Local Sources of help and   Useful addresses
    advice   Useful books and leaflets

Throughout this book we have suggested where you should go for help and advice. This chapter brings all these suggestions together as a reference source.

Local sources of help and advice

Job Centres
Your Job Centre is a mine of information on all sorts of matters, including the address of your local Enterprise Agency, Enterprise Allowances available, recruitment and local government grants. Their services are free.

Government Departments
The Department of Employment, the Department of Trade and Industry and the Department of Social Security all have an interest in small businesses. Your local offices of these departments have leaflets available on all sorts of subjects. The Inland Revenue and HM Customs and Excise are also willing to give help and advice.

Enterprise Agencies
These are there to help you take the first steps. They will listen to

your ideas and advise you on where to contact solicitors, bankers, accountants and so on. They also have information on training courses available, grants and allowances, and some run their own training courses.

Colleges
Many colleges run courses in conjunction with the Training Agency and the Enterprise Agency to help you get your business off the ground. They usually welcome people anxious to set up on their own, and sometimes run a Small Business Club. You do not need any qualifications to join their courses, (not even GCSEs or 'O' Levels) unless they are in very specialised areas – just apply and join.

Banks and Building Societies
These financial organisations are very willing to listen to people starting their own business, but of course they are selling their own wares, so shop around.

Public libraries
If you have a good library with an informative and well-stocked reference section, use it. The librarians know what they have got on their shelves. Use their knowledge and expertise to your advantage.

Useful addresses

BOTB (British Overseas Trade Board)   071 215 7877
Marketing and Briefing Unit
1 Victoria Street
London SW1H 0ET

British Franchise Association   0491 578049
75a Bell Street
Henley-on-Thames
Oxon RG9 2BD

Companies Registration Office (CRO)   0222 388588
Companies House
Crown Way
Maindy
Cardiff

Department of Trade and Industry   071 215 7877
10–18 Victoria Street
London SW1H 0NM

Electronic Mail Networks
    Datalink   0532 442219
    Mercury Link 7500   081 847 6070
    One-to-one   071 351 2468
    Telecom Gold   071 403 6777

The Industrial Society   071 839 4300
3 Carlton House Terrace
London SW1

InterChange   071 267 9421
15 Wilkin Street
London NW5 3NG

National Co-operative Development   071 839 2988
    Agency
Broadmead House
21 Panton Street
London SW1 4DR

SITPRO (Simplification of   071 930 0532
    International Trade Procedures Board)
Almack House
26–28 King Street
London SW1Y 3QW

Useful books and leaflets

A Shop of Your Own
Kogan Page
120 Pentonville Road,
    London N1
(071 278 0433)

Booklet HS(R)S
Health and Safety Executive
Regina House

Old Marylebone Road, London
    NW1
(071 229 3456)

*Croners Reference Book for
    Employers*
Croner Publications Ltd
173 Kingston Road,
New Malden, Surrey KT3 3SS
(081 942 8966)

*Employing Other People in the
    Small Business*
ACAS
Clifton House, Euston Road,
    London NW1
(071 388 5100)

*Employing People in the Small
    Business*
Job Centre

English Language Skills
Vera Hughes
Macmillan
Houndmills, Basingstoke,
    Hants. RG21 2XS
(0256 29242)

Estate Agents
Kogan Page

Export for the Small Business
Henry Deschampsneufs
Kogan Page

First Aid Manual
British Red Cross Society, St
    John Ambulance Brigade,
St Andrew's Ambulance
    Association

*Importing for the Small
    Business*
Mag Morris
Kogan Page

*Marketing Tools for the Small
    Business*
M. Gowland
Marketing for Enterprise,
    38 Shaw Road, Stockport,
    Cheshire SK4 4AE
(061 442 5147)

People in Retailing
Vera Hughes and David Weller
Macmillan

Profitable Retailing
Vera Hughes and David Weller
Macmillan

*Teach Yourself The Office
    Handbook*
Vera and Christina Hughes
Hodder and Stoughton, Mill
    Road, Dunton Green,
    Sevenoaks, Kent TN13 2YA

Which? Tax-saving Guide
Which? Publications
2 Marylebone Road,
London NW1 4DX

Index

A
ACAS 119
Access for customers 19
Access for goods 20
– factories 23
– shops 129
– warehouses 23
– workshops 23
Accident Book 123
Accommodation
– offices 26
Accountant 17, 83
– qualifications 32
Accounts software 104
Additional sales (selling
    sequence) 59
Advertisements 41
Advertising
– for staff 115
– shops 137–139
Advertising matter
– image 50
– leaflets 138
Advice Note 144
AIDA 41, 46, 138
Airmail Transfer 145
Air Waybill 144
Allowable expenses 77–81
– women 163
Amex 75
Analysis of payments 63

Application forms 116
Approach (selling sequence) 53
Architects 83
Articles of Association 32
Artwork 47
Assets 13
– current 14
Au pairs (women) 156

B
Banking 70–72
Bank Statements 71
Banker's Order 145
Banks 16, 84, 169
Benefits (selling sequence) 55
Bill of Exchange 146
Bill of Lading 144
Bills 93
Book-keeping 2, 62, 83
Book-keeping software 104
British Franchise Association,
    The 34
British Overseas Trade Board
    (BOTB) 147
Building Societies 17, 84, 169
Buildings insurance 87
Business
– cards 93
– documents 94
– Plan 15, 17
– routine 4

C
Cables 104
C&F (Cost and Freight) 147
Camera-ready copy (CRC) 88
Capital Gains Tax 22
Car expenses (women) 164
Cash
– flow 13
– Flow Forecast 14–15, 17, 73, 83
– withdrawal 84
Cash and Carry Wholesalers 94
Central Processing Unit (CPU)
      103
Charity Commissioners 34
Cheques
– bouncing 85
– company 84
Childminders (women) 156
Children (women) 154
Cleaning 22
Clearing Agent 144
Closed questions 55
Closing (selling sequence) 58
Colleges 169
Communication skills 8
– spoken 8
– written 9
Community Charge 22
Companies Registration Office 32
Competition 2, 16
Competitors 129
Compliments slips 92
Computer
– materials 104
– packages 103
– suppliers 105
Computers 73, 101
Consultancy 19
– marketing 48
Consumer protection legislation
      134
Contents Insurance 87
Contracts of Employment 120
Conveyancing 89
Co-operatives 34
Costing 11

– product 11
– service 11
Cost Insurance Freight (CIF) 147
Cost price 11
Cottage industry 19
Credit cards 75
Credit Note 99
Creditors 13
Credit Transfers 84
Current assets 14
Current liabilities 14
Customer
– access 19
– establishing needs (selling
      sequence) 54
Customs 144

D
Data Protection Act 121
Debtors 13
Decor (shops) 131
Dependents (women) 158
Desktop publishing (DTP) 88
– software 104
Development Areas 29
Diners Club 75
Directors' fees 65
Disciplinary Procedure 121
Disks 104
Dismissal 121
Drawings 65
DSS 30, 31
DTI 29, 36

E
Electronic Mail 107
Email 107
Employers' Liability Insurance
      87, 122
Employing others 114
Employment law 89
Energy 7
Enterprise Agency 2, 168
Enterprise Zones 29
Envelopes 92
Equipment 20, 108

Establishing customer needs
    (selling sequence) 54
Estate Agents 27, 85
Estimate 94
Eye strain and VDUs 111
Expenses 75
– allowable 77–81
Experienced Worker Standard
    (EWS) 125
Export 147

F
Factories 22
– access 23
– cost 25
– health and safety 24
– security 24
– size 23
Fair Trading Act 36
Fax 106
Features and benefits (selling
    sequence) 55
Financial Services Act 86
First aid 123
Fixed assets 13
Fixtures and fittings 130
Franchise 33
– advantages 33
– disadvantages 33
Franking machine 108
Free on Board (FOB) 146
Funding 16
Furniture 107

G
Goods access 20
Goods in Transit Insurance 87
Government
– departments 168
– grants 28
– support 28
Grievance Procedure 122

H
Hardware 103
HASAWA 24, 110, 123

Headed paper 91
Health 7
– checks 8
– women 158–160
– and safety 24
Health and Safety Executive
    111
Help and advice 168
HM Customs & Excise 69–70, 83,
    86, 144
Holiday Pay 120
Home and business (women)
    150–154

I
Image 26, 48
– advertising matter 50
– letters 49
– office premises 26
– personnel 50
– shops 130
– telephone 49
– vehicles 49
– women 160–163
Import 143
Import and Export 142
Income Tax 76, 119
Industrial Tribunal 121
Inland Revenue 30, 31, 76
Insurance
– brokers 86
– companies 17
– imports 146
Insurances 87, 122
Interchange 35
Interest 12
Invoice 96
Invoiced Sales 65

J
Job
– Centre 2, 168
– Description 117
– interviews 118
– offers 118
– Specification 116

K
KISS 42

L
Labels 92
Labour 11
Law Centre 89
Leads 47
Leaflet drops 44
Leaflets (shops) 138
Leasing 89
Letter of Credit 145
Letters 101
– image 49
Liabilities 13
– current 14
Libraries 27, 169
Life Insurance 87
Lighting and heating 22
Lighting (shops) 131
Limited Company 32
Loading 24
Local Authorities 28
Local Authority Grants 28
Local Authority support 28
Local Enterprise Agencies
    (LEAs) 28, 82
Loss of Earnings Insurance 87

M
Machinery 11
Mailshots 42
Management of time 4
Margin 12
Marketing 2, 39
– methods 40
– need 2
– profile 39
– segment 2
– strategy 2, 16
Market research 2
Mark Up 12
Materials 11
Maternity
– pay 120
– rights 119

Memorandum of Association 32
Merchant Bankers 17
Methods of paying staff 118
Methods of payment abroad 145
Methods of trading 30
– limited company 32
– multi-level marketing 36
– partnership 31
– registered charity 34
– sole trader 30
Misunderstandings (selling
    sequence) 56
Money
– for personal use 75
– shops 134
– women 163
Mother's Help (women) 156

N
Nannies (women) 154
National Cooperative
    Development Agency 34
National Insurance (NI) 76, 119
Near Letter Quality (NLQ) 103

O
Objections (selling sequence) 56
Office 91
– premises 25
– accommodation 26
– image 26
– services 26
Offices, Shops and Railway
    Premises Act 26, 134
Opening day (shops) 139
Opening Hours (shops) 132
Open questions 54
Order 96
Order Book 93
Ordering from abroad 143
Organisational ability 4
Overdraft 13
Overheads 12, 21

P
P45 119
P60 119

Paper 92
– computer 105
Pay 118
Pay back period 17
Payments 63
– analysis 63
Parking 23
Partnership 31
Partnership Agreement 31, 89
PBX (Private Branch Exchange) 106
Pensions
– employees 120
– personal 76
Period of Notice 122
Personal
– attributes 3
– contacts 47
– finances 75
– service (shops) 130
Personal Pension Plan (PPP) 76
Personnel
– image 50
– shops 133
Petty Cash 66–67
Photocopier 109
Pilot Scheme 9
Planning Permission
– legal 89
– plans 83
Planning restrictions 86
Poll Tax 22
Post Office 43
Pregnancy and VDUs 111
Premises 19, 86
– image 49
– security (shops) 137
Preparation (selling sequence) 52
Press Release 48, 138
Price (selling sequence) 57
Printers 87
Printing 47
Print wheels 105
Product 1
– costing 11

Professional Negligence Insurance 87
Professionals 82
Professions 79
Pro Forma Invoice 144
Public Liability Insurance 87
Public Relations (PR) 48
Purpose of business 16

Q
Questions
– closed 55
– open 54
Quotation 96
QWERTY keyboard 103

R
Rates 129
Raw materials 3
Receipts 62
Records 72
Redundancy 122
Registered Charity 34
Remittance Advice 99
Rent 25, 129
Rental Agreements 89
Ribbons 104
Routine 21

S
Sale of Goods Act 134
Scepticism (selling sequence) 57
Schedule of Duties 117
Secretarial services 88
Security 22, 24
– moneys 72, 136
– shops 135–137
– stock 136
Self discipline 4, 21
Self motivation 3
Selling 2
– price 13
– sequence 52
SERPS 76
Service 1
– costing 11

Services
- office 26
Shops 127
- self service 130
- siting 127
- size and shape 128
- stock 131
- stocktaking 132
- suppliers 132
Sick Pay 120
SITPRO (Simplification of
    International Trade
    Procedures Board) 148
Software 103
Sole Trader 30
Solicitors 88
Space 20
Special Cover Insurance 87
Spellchecker 104
Spoken communication skills 8
Spread Sheets 104
Staff
- recruitment 115
- selection 115
- training 124–125
Standing Orders 84
Statement (of Account) 99
Stationery 49, 91
- design 93
- image 49
- suppliers 94
Statutory Holidays 120
Statutory Sick Pay (SSP) 119
Storage space 20
SWIFT 145
Sub-letting 89
Suppliers 3, 132
Surveys 83

T
Taxes 12
- Capital Gains 22
- Community Charge 22
- Poll Tax 22
- VAT 22

Tax Returns 83
Teaching 19
Telecommunications 105
Telegraphic Transfer 145
Telephone 22, 105
- image 49
Teletex 106
Telex 106
Thomsons Directory 82
Trades Description Act 134
Trading Account 83
Training 19, 124–125
- women 165
Training Agency 2
Time management 4
- discipline 6
- guidelines 5
- operating 5
- planning 5
- telephone control 6
- travelling 7

U
Unloading 23
Useful addresses 169

V
VAT 22, 31, 57, 68–69
- calculations 69
- Office 86
- on imports 145
- receipts 67
- registration 30, 68
- Returns 69, 73, 83
VDUs 111
Vehicles
- image 49
- insure 87
Visual aids 46

W
Wages and salaries 13
Warehouses 22
- access 23
- cost 25
- Health and Safety 24

– security 24
– size 23
Women 150
– organisations 165
– training 165
Word processing software 103
Working Capital 13, 14
Working from home 19
– advantages 22
– disadvantages 22
Workshops 22

– access 23
– cost 25
– Health and Safety 24
– security 24
– size 23
Workstation design 111
Written communication skills 9

Y
Year End 74
Yellow Pages Directory 42, 47, 82